How to
Sleep Alone
in a
King-Size Bed

A Memoir of Starting Over

How to Sleep Alone in a King-Size Bed

Theo Pauline Nestor

 THREE RIVERS PRESS • NEW YORK

Reading Group Guide copyright © 2009 by Three Rivers Press, an imprint of
the Crown Publishing Group, a division of Random House, Inc., New York.

Library of Congress Cataloging-in-Publication Data
  Nestor, Theo Pauline.
    How to sleep alone in a king-size bed : a memoir of
starting over. Theo Pauline Nestor.—1st ed.
      1. Nestor, Theo Pauline. 2. Divorced women—
Biography. I. Title.
  HQ814.N45   2007
  306.89'3092—dc22
  [B]   2007041074

ISBN 978-0-307-34677-3

Printed in the United States of America

DESIGN BY BARBARA STURMAN

10 9 8 7 6 5 4

First Paperback Edition

For my mother and my stepfather

Contents

A NOTE FROM THE AUTHOR

My life is bound up with the lives of the people dear to me, some of whom would not have chosen to have their stories told at this time or, perhaps, in this way. Because I cannot tell my story without telling parts of theirs, I have changed several of the names and identifying characteristics of the people in this book to protect their privacy. The conversations here have been reconstructed from memory and may differ from others' memories of those same conversations. I am grateful to my inner circle of family and friends for allowing me to portray them in my version of these events.

Part One

Shock and Denial

"How did you go bankrupt?" Bill asked. "Two ways," Mike said. "Gradually and then suddenly."

—ERNEST HEMINGWAY, *The Sun Also Rises*

Things Fall Apart

Some marriages grind to a halt; two tired people lock down into a final frozen position like the wheels of rusty gears that refuse at last to mesh again. Other marriages, like mine, blow apart midflight, torn asunder by forces larger than themselves, viewers watching numbly as the networks broadcast the final surreal seconds over and over again.

It's late September, a time when Seattle always seems so easy and forgiving, as though you'll forever be padding barefoot out to the garden for a handful of basil and rosemary, as though the skies will never turn gray and close down around you. It's warm still, but past the last hot days of Indian summer. I've waited for this day for at least half the summer——a day cool enough to roast a chicken. When I put our five-pound chicken in the oven, a shower of fresh green herbs clinging to its breast, I am married. As far as I know, nothing is wrong, or at least not *really* wrong. By the time I pull this chicken out of the oven, I will have asked my husband to leave our house, and he'll have driven away with his green car stuffed with clothes slipping off their hangers.

Last night we went to sleep beside each other as we have for the last twelve years, neither of us knowing it would be for the last time. Could I have seen this coming? I ask myself this now, and I realize that I might have, had I been watching rather than living, had I not been scrambling to and from Jess's preschool and Natalie's science fair and the Children's Theater portrayal of *Go, Dog. Go!,* had I not been writing and teaching part-time at the university and squeezing in walks around Green Lake with my friends.

But even if I hadn't been busy with all that, I probably wouldn't have sat still, still enough to realize that something *was* wrong, to say to myself: There's a reason why you feel this way. That nagging feeling that you've misplaced something or that you're working too hard to hold the universe together—that's real. You've felt it before, long ago, when you were too young to know the words for all the ways that life could go wrong. You've gotten too used to that barely audible hum of doubt. And now, here it is again. Quiet. Listen. It's the voice of that part of you that hasn't missed a thing.

At four-thirty, the chicken's in the oven, and I'm waiting for Kevin to return with Natalie from soccer practice. Jessica is sitting at the counter, mashing Play-Doh into patties, while I pace around the kitchen trying to figure out something I'm refusing to see. I have this sinking feeling something is wrong, and it has to do with money. It's odd how I can be obsessed with a problem—scouring bank statements and frantically pawing through bills—yet blind to the real source of the trouble. The thing is, Kevin has been very busy with his real estate business these past few months, but he still hasn't made any real money. It's nothing we haven't seen before in his business—a deal falls apart, a commission is unexpectedly reduced—but this time things just don't add up; the busier he gets, the less money he seems to make. But every time I try to crack the code of where all the money is going, one of the kids asks whether we can go for ice cream or to the park and the facts and numbers slip back into the fuzzy abyss that I've come to consider Kevin's half of our family's concerns.

I decide to call the bank once again to confirm the balance on my checking account. A hundred dollars was withdrawn from a nearby ATM two nights before at midnight. But I know that's impossible—we were all in bed on Sunday at midnight. I remembered we all watched *Daddy Day Care* in the big bed and had the kids asleep in their bunks by nine. So I cancel the card and ask the nice customer service person to start a fraud report. Then I look again in my wallet. How can the card be in my wallet if someone else used it? Does someone have my bank card number? Is it identity theft? My mother sends me at least one article a week on identity theft, which I promptly recycle, and I've always suspected that my punishment for not reading them would eventually be to have my identity stolen.

At 4:53 I'm staring at the broken red lines of the numbers on the microwave clock when a cold knowledge floods through me like a glacial thawing. I know now that this has to do with Kevin. Sunday night starts to come back to me in patches. I'd gone to sleep right after the kids, but Kevin had gone downstairs to watch TV. Like many nights, I had no idea what time he'd crawled into bed beside me. He's always been a night owl, and lately going to bed at separate times has seemed like a brilliant arrangement, as there's been this constant low-level friction between us. The least little irritating comment by one of us, things we might've shaken off years ago, can ignite a hopeless argument that is simultaneously about nothing and about everything, both shockingly trivial and terrifyingly serious. But in a long marriage, it gets pretty hard to tell what's serious and what's not: what's you, what's the other person, and what's just life. Sometimes we get along really well, and sometimes we don't. The bad stretches are misery, but it's the kind of ordinary misery that you'd expect from any marathon endeavor, the price of togetherness. We came close to breaking up once years ago and weathered that, so I've always assumed that—unless something terrible happens—we'll be married at least until the kids are grown. With two kids still in elementary school, I don't have the presence of mind to fathom what life might look like after their high school graduations. It's like life on other planets; maybe it's there, but you really can't picture it.

But now I know that it was after midnight on Sunday when he came to bed, probably well after. I don't know the details yet, but I feel the enormity of the situation with my whole body.

When they finally arrive, at ten after five, Natalie clomps up the front stairs first in her soccer cleats. She wants to know if she can watch *Arthur*. As I nod yes to her and she scrambles upstairs, I stare at Kevin. I'm thinking that if I stare hard enough I might be able to see right through him to the secrets he's been keeping, but I can't. A poker face, they call it. He's trained himself to bluff and not show it—at the card table and with me.

"We need to talk," I say in an ominous tone, hoping I can scare a confession out of him. But I've grossly underestimated how long and how deeply he's held this secret, and how determined he is to hang on to it.

We walk back into our daughters' room and I close the door. I sit on the desk chair and he's hunched over on the bottom bunk. Behind him, pensive fairies in gossamer gowns float by on the wallpaper, a persistent promise of security from a world where picking a cabbage rose is the tallest order of the day. Wallpapering the girls' room was the first thing we did four years ago when we bought this hundred-year-old house.

"I think you have something to tell me," I begin.

"No, I don't," he says quickly.

This seems like a strange and suspicious reply. Wouldn't an innocent person say something more like, "What in the hell are you talking about?" I notice that there are very dark circles under his eyes. I realize now that I've seen them before but not registered them, in that peculiar way you can see but not register changes on those faces you know exceedingly well, like your own or the face of the person to whom you've been married for more than a decade.

I confront him with the withdrawal from the bank and he denies knowing anything about it. His face, though, looks ashen and drawn, and suddenly I realize that my hunch is right. I know, too, that there's a lot more to this—more than I want to know.

I know that he remembers what I said to him five years ago, when I opened a credit card bill for $5,000 he'd secretly gambled away. I was pregnant with our younger daughter, Jessica, then, and I told him that was the last time I could endure a break in trust. If it happened again, I said, I would have to get a divorce. To save our marriage and try to rebuild trust, we went to couples therapy and set up new "safety measures": He'd give me his commission checks to keep in a separate account, and he'd call me more often to tell me where he was and when he'd be home.

How did we get to this desolate place? How did I lose this person who once was my closest friend?

I decide to bluff. "The woman at the bank said that when they run the fraud report, they can bring up photos from the ATM. They'll be able to tell who used my card last Sunday at midnight."

He holds his breath for a second and then says, "Okay, so big deal. I took the money from your account."

I look at him, trying to record these new facts: A few nights ago he waited for me to go to sleep, went downstairs, took the bank card from my purse, drove to the bank, entered my PIN, withdrew the hundred dollars, then came home and returned the card to my purse, and went to sleep beside me.

I can't. And I can't believe that this is the person I'm married to. But some part of me knows it's true and knows that there's more bad news ahead. She's the one who says, "You're gambling again."

He admits that he is, but he won't admit the details or how much he's lost. It will be days before I learn that he has charged tens of thousands of dollars we don't have to charge cards I knew nothing about, that the cards are stashed in the glove compartment of his car and the bills sent to another address, and by then he will be holed up in a motel a few miles away, never coming back to live in our house again. In fact, he will be gone before I even have time to absorb what has happened, even before the juice from the thigh of the chicken "no longer runs pink," to quote one of my favorite cookbooks.

At 6:00 p.m., with the September sun on the wane, the roasted chicken—burnt rosemary stems like black twigs now scoring the breast—sits neglected on the counter. The chicken feeds only one person that night—our nine-year-old daughter, Natalie. I'm not hungry anymore. In fact, the chicken looks strangely unfamiliar, a dinner dropped into my kitchen by aliens perhaps.

Our five-year-old daughter, Jessie, says she won't eat a chicken that looks like a chicken, but would possibly eat five chicken nuggets from the box in the freezer. For once, I don't argue, "But all this good food is going to waste." The waste has already happened. I take the red box from the freezer, pluck out five tawny nuggets and place them on a plate, heat them for forty-seven seconds in the microwave, and set them with a fork and napkin in front of Jessie, who believes that her father has gone to meet a friend downtown and that the two of them will be leaving tonight on an impromptu car trip. It is a ludicrous story. A last-minute trip with a friend who lives two thousand miles away but has, apparently, just arrived downtown unexpectedly? Yet the children believe me, and I hate myself a little already. "Dad will come home in a week," I tell them. But I know he won't. He won't ever come home.

How did you lose your husband? I ask myself.

At first slowly and then all at once.

2

The Girl and Her Mother

One of the first calls I make is to my mother. I call her before I can talk myself out of it, punch in her numbers so quickly and so instinctively that I'm a little startled when she actually answers.

I tell her something is horribly wrong but the children are okay.

"What is it?" she asks, and I can feel her holding her breath and I know—because I am also a mother—how afraid she is of what will come next.

"We're getting *divorced*," I say. The word comes out long and mangled, a high-pitched animal sound.

"Are you sure?" she asks.

I say I am.

"Okay, then," she says. "You're going to be okay, dear. You really will be."

I'm surprised to find myself believing this the way a child

believes her mother when she tells her the skinned knee will heal or that she'll someday forget about the boy who turned her down. I wait for her to talk me out of it, to say maybe things can be worked out, or the dreaded refrain of "men will be men," but she doesn't, and my relief is instant. She just takes me at my word. If I say it's over, then it must be.

In some ways it's as if we're on equal footing at last. Marriage on the rocks—this is her territory, and her role has transformed in the last two minutes from outsider to guide, a role neither of us thought she'd fill again for me. But the change isn't just in her; in the instant that I know she has heard and accepted my decision, I feel something shift in me. It's as though tectonic plates are converging, and a new landscape, as yet imperceptible, has begun forming. Ten million years might pass before there's a mountain range here, but deep below ground the earth changes irrevocably each time continents collide. And some part of me has begun to trust my mother to help me.

My graduate school and professional days behind me—and now my life as a married woman as well—I'm finally about to enter into the kind of life my mother can understand. It makes sense that the daughter's life should look like the mother's, that the daughter has not outstripped her mother. I may not like it, but there's a primal logic to it. By the time my mom was my age—forty-two—she had three kids and was on the verge of her third marriage, which would eventually end, like the others, in divorce. She knows what it's like to pay the bills alone, go to bed alone, and get up in the night alone to feed the baby. She knows what it's like to watch things fall apart.

My parents were ahead of the curve, divorcing in 1962 when the divorce rate was at the low it had fallen to during World War II, when people were too busy fighting our enemies overseas to think about their domestic battles. In 1962, American women were, for the most part, standing by their men and cutting the crusts off white-bread sandwiches for afternoon tea parties. Just ten years later, women would be leaving their husbands like crazy to become Realtors or lawyers or interior decorators, but in 1967 my elementary school still had enough confidence in the nuclear family to host a Daddy/Daughter Pancake Breakfast, knowing that most of the little girls had a dad at home they could drag in on a Saturday morning.

There was something in the culture of my family that made divorce acceptable, a reasonable preemptive strike in the struggle for self-actualization. I grew up surrounded by conversations about ex-husbands and ex-wives, words that sounded as ordinary to me as *uncle* or *cousin*. There were no examples of Happily Ever After or even Sticking It Out in my family. Not only my mother but both my grandmothers had been married multiple times, having left their first husbands before their twenty-second birthdays. My father's mother, JoJo, raised on stock-market money and Ralph Waldo Emerson, had unveiled contempt for conformists who weren't hip to the fact that the highest of all callings is one's own personal happiness.

Our family tree has been so twisted and truncated by divorce that it's impossible to map it with the usual flow-chart. There would have to be a great number of crossing arrows, footnotes, and lengthy annotations, explaining who was raised by whom, and who is whose stepsister or half-brother. We bleed into other families when they raise our children or when the father from one family comes to be our father for a while. There is no *us*.

And yet somehow we've survived to eke out another generation.

It began like this: Almost a hundred years ago two women were born in different parts of the world—one in London and the other in San Diego. Both of these women, unbeknownst to themselves, belonged to the same tribe—the live-free-or-die women. One came of age, tanned and boyish, in first Southern and then Northern California; the other, pale and retiring, left her native England for the frigid wheat plains of Canada, then moved to its western coast, rainy and thick with firs. The women married in their teens, as did many young women in the 1920s. Each had a child before her twentieth birthday: for the pale Canadian, Madge, a blue-eyed girl, Diane; for the tanned Californian, Josephine, a dark-eyed boy, Jack.

Then the two women strode away from the path that was mapped out for them and other women of their era. Now it was 1930. The stock market had taken its plunge. Men in suits and white shirts stood in line for things that were once theirs for the taking—food, jobs, chances. And these two women, my grandmothers, stepped out onto a precipice jutting into a future where women would raise children however they could instead of how everyone thought they must. They ditched their husbands. *They* left. They decided they'd had enough, and they went. Their toddlers, pulling on mittens and wet swimming trunks, kept up with them as best they could.

In the thirties and forties, through the Depression and war, my grandmothers raised their children with new husbands, stepfathers who did and did not love these refugee children as their own. In Canada, husband Walter doted on stepdaughter Diane. In California, new husband Charlie beat little Jack. I remember my grandmother JoJo saying, "With all those millions of people who died in World War II, why did Charlie Nestor have to come home?"

In the sixties the grandkids would be dropped at JoJo's for an occasional weekend. She was willing to take us, one at a time, after we hit the age of eight or so. Kids younger than that annoyed her, diverting her attention too often from whatever she was creating that week. We'd stay at her little pink stucco house just south of San Francisco, with the lime trees lining the driveway, making batiks and tie-dyes of magenta and turquoise in plastic buckets in her backyard, which had made the pages of *Sunset* magazine more than once. She was a landscape architect, and sometimes we'd go with her to job sites and hold the surveyor's rod while she looked through the funny telescope, occasionally barking, "God damn it, child. Stay still!"

Once we were eating potato salad at the picnic table that served as her dining room table, and she looked up at me and said, very crossly, "You can have material things or you can have freedom. You have to choose." I must have been about nine. My grandmother had already lived alone for more than a decade in her little bungalow filled with crazy art.

"Why choose?" I asked.

"Because if you don't choose, you'll end up with things and you'll be stuck."

"Stuck?"

"Yep. Most people are, do you realize that?" She seemed very angry now, as if she herself were being held against her will.

"But you're not, are you?" I couldn't really understand what she meant, but I didn't want to make her angrier, or for her to direct her anger at me.

"No, I'm not. And I never will be. But you, it could happen to you."

"No, it won't," I said and then looking at her and, realizing I hadn't satisfied her yet, I swallowed a lump of potato salad and added, "I won't let it."

IT STARTS WITH A HOLE IN A SOCK, NO BIG DEAL REALLY. But then it begins to irk me that my toe is sticking out, cold and exposed. My kids are off at school and the house resounds with that eerie midweek, midday quiet. The city outside my window hums with the low-level roar of the business week, an incessant reminder that people everywhere are busy engaging in art, commerce, and education while I'm here pulling old socks out of my dresser.

But this is my work this morning—to get myself dressed and to the grocery store—so I try another pair and then another. Some have holes by the big toe, some by the pinky toe. But they all have holes. Why? What's wrong with me that I have no two socks that are both matching and without holes? Suddenly it's just too much to bear that I'm for sure getting a divorce and that I for sure have not one pair of socks to wear that doesn't make me look like an orphan.

As a child I always had the wrong socks. My nemesis was a pair of perennially drooping ankle socks so loose at the top that no sooner were they up than they slid down again, exposing my heel and bunching into a mass under the arch of my foot. With every step all I could think was, My socks are sliding down, my socks are sliding down. It never occurred to me to ask my mother for new or different socks. Sometimes I'd fish the slack cotton up past the T-strap of my Mary Janes and thread them once again up and over the heel and up my ankle, but moments later one was sure to slide down again. Soon after, the other would follow. Eventually I'd give up the struggle and endure the day with part of my consciousness trained on my bare heels, never fully able to give myself to the task ahead, always certain that there was something not quite right about me.

I sit down on the floor beside my bed. It's been just two weeks since Kevin and I split up. I'm taking care of so many details to keep the legal separation proceedings aloft and maintain the kids' lives that the idea of getting in the car and driving to the store and getting out of the car and walking into the store and choosing the right socks and paying for the right socks and driving home with the right socks in the bag beside me seems an insurmountable task, like health-care reform or time travel. I shake a holey sock in my fist and cry out loud, "I need help."

Luckily I've fallen into the hands of a good therapist. She said something last week about asking for the help I need, and I grumbled. In some ways I see myself as someone who already asks for help. I've asked people to hold doors open when my arms were full; I've asked strangers to jump-start my car when the battery died; I asked my husband to help me clean the house. But I've never asked someone for something I wanted very badly that I didn't think they'd want to give.

I call my mom again.

"There's something I need."

"Some money?" she asks. My mom has always been extremely generous about writing checks. You need only to whisper the word *money* and she has her checkbook out. Most parents of grown children—at least most of my friends' parents—don't seem to be like this. They want their children to be constantly learning about bootstraps and self-reliance. My mom's smart enough to know that I'm not about to learn any new lessons right now and that being broke with kids leads more often to despair than to self-improvement.

"Well, yes, that, but something else, too. I need you to buy me a nice pair of socks that fit me. Not socks on sale, but some *really good quality socks*. Like I'm thinking top shelf here. And then I need you to put them in a mailing envelope, go to a post office, and send them to me."

My mom's silent for an extra beat. These are a lot of steps for someone who typically doesn't do more at Christmas than send a check for the grandkids with the instructions, "Go buy them something nice, wrap it up, and tell them it's from me."

"Socks? You're saying you want a pair of socks?"

"Yes. That's right."

"Honey, I'll just send you some money and you can go pick out whatever socks you want."

"But that's not what I need from you."

"Oh. Okay."

I can feel her getting quieter. I sense her listening more closely. My courage gathers. "Mom, get a pen. There are some things I need you to get me."

"Okay, a list. Let's see here, a pen. Okay, shoot." One of my mom's points of pride is that she always has a pen by the phone. If she tells me an address or a phone number over the phone and I say, "Hold on. I need a pen," she'll say, "You don't have one by the phone?"

"Number one: socks."

"How many pairs?"

"Let's say three."

"Five?" she asks, her voice hopeful.

"Okay, five."

"Ankle or knee?"

"Okay, good you asked. This is very, very important. You see, Mom, I don't want ankle. I only want kneesocks. And they must stay up but not be too tight. There's a very thin line between socks that stay up and those that choke you at the knee."

"Okay," she says, in the style of a secretary in an old movie taking dictation from her very important boss. I could see her scratching away with the pen, the phone crooked between her shoulder and her ear. "Stay uu-p, but not ti-ght. Is that right?"

"Yes."

"Okay. What else?"

"What else? Like you'd go get anything for me?"

"Well, yes. I guess I would, within reason. Yes, what else do you need?"

"When I was little, you got me *Tiger Beat* magazines and ginger ale when I was sick."

"But you don't want those now, do you?" she says, laughing.

"No, but I want to feel like that. Like I can stay in bed and get well and you will get me what I need and it won't be any trouble for you. You will want to do it."

"I do want to. I want to help you." She's starting to sniff a little.

"Okay, keep writing. I need a bottle of Advil—Extra Strength, a king-size bottle. And some liquid Children's

Advil, the bubble-gum flavor—not cherry, the kids hate the cherry. If they get a fever in the night, I'm gonna need that. It's not like there's one person to run to the drugstore and another to stay home anymore. And I need some underwear and I need a tube of Clinique makeup—Mom, this is going to mean two stores. To get the Clinique, you'll have to go to the department store at the mall. Is that okay? I mean it'll be two stores *and* the post office. That's three stops. In and out of the car each time, right?"

"It's okay."

"Okay. This has to be just right. It's called Clinique Almost Makeup and the shade is Medium."

"Almost Makeup is the product name. Clinique is the brand," she says, a bit like a first-grader who's just learned the difference between a city and a state.

"That's right."

"Got it," she says. And, perhaps for the first time, I know she really does.

The box arrives by FedEx two days later, and I steal off to my room so I can open it alone. I slice the packing tape with a kitchen knife, and the socks appear first. They're perfect—smooth white brushed cotton with a ribbing that promises to stay at the knee. Whatever I have to deal with today—bad phone calls from Kevin, an evening alone with the kids that threatens to stretch from the dinner dishes into infinity—my socks are going to be right. And with those socks right, some part of my mind will know that someone in the world loves me enough to make sure my feet are covered. All the other goodies are in there, too, and they're exactly what I'd asked for, right down to the bubble-gum flavor and the king-size bottle. The feeling of being taken care of is so profound I feel a bit dizzy. My mother is helping me in the very specific ways I requested, and I'm letting her. I pull on my new socks and sit on the floor wondering if anything short of a divorce could have broken down the wall I have built between us.

And then I spot something. There, stuffed between socks and underwear and over-the-counter medications, are a couple of items I hadn't asked for—a Starbucks gift card and some fancy chocolates, the grown-up equivalents of ginger ale and *Tiger Beat* magazine.

My mother has long understood that a woman's mastery over her own destiny is a tenuous thing. Throughout my adolescence, her chant was this: Don't marry young, don't get pregnant, and whatever you do, don't marry young. When pressed for an explanation, she assumed a faraway look and said, with airy despondency, "When a man and woman are very young, there are things they can't know." This conjured up for me the image of the wholesomely naked man and woman who embraced on the Trojans package, or the similar couple that appeared in my copy of *Our Bodies, Ourselves,* which I thumbed through nightly like a prayer book.

And what were these *things* they couldn't know, I wondered with impatience, and why couldn't they just ask someone or look them up and then get on with the business of being happy? But my mother kept it all in the abstract and changed the subject quickly, as if this advice against marriage and motherhood weren't grounded in her own experience of having been abandoned at nineteen by her first husband while she was still in the first trimester of her first pregnancy.

These conversations with my mother must have taken place around the time I turned sixteen and started having sex. During one of those early episodes with my boyfriend, I remember thinking with each thrust, I could get pregnant, I could get pregnant. After months of passionate make-out sessions, of tangled clothes and chins rubbed raw from kissing, I woke into a stony sobriety. As my body pushed numbly against his, a 3-D version of the glossy Health Ed booklets reeled in my vigilant mind—ambitious sperm sped up the dark tunnel and invaded the naïve egg that lay in wait, suspended in a hazy triangle of pink.

"What's wrong?" he asked, freezing midstroke above me.

"Nothing," I lied.

"You're not into it, are you?"

"No, it's fine, just keep going."

"Keep going? I don't want to do this by myself. This isn't algebra class." He was an engineering student at the university, but he tended to use high-school examples when he wanted to make a point with me, the sixteen-year-old.

"Okay, okay. I could get pregnant. I can't stop thinking that, you know."

"The condom, remember?"

"Yeah, but it could happen. It could." I pulled myself out from under him.

He went quiet, his face sinking into a serious expression as his eyes cast about his boyhood room, landing first on a map of the solar system and then on a dusty rock collection.

"I'd marry you," he said, a hand stroking my shoulder.

"What?" In one swift movement, I had wrapped myself in the comforter and leapt from the bed, leaving him exposed, his penis now deflated in the waxy-looking condom.

"You don't think I would, but I will. We'd get an apartment. I'd quit school if I had to."

The idea of being the pregnant child-bride of an engineering student—nay, gas station attendant—had me pulling on my jeans and cramming my feet into my still-tied sneakers. "I don't want to get *married*." I spat out the word like it was something stuck to my tongue.

"Not yet, you mean?" He had the comforter now. It was slung around his shoulders so he looked more like an old man in a convalescent home than like a university student. "But after university, right?"

"I don't know. University? Am I even going? I don't know. No. Not ever. I don't ever want to get married." It occurred to me then that I probably should have thought about this before, but really I hadn't. I did have the vague sense that I would someday lead a Mary Tyler Moore sort of existence— a small apartment, a small career—but I hadn't formulated any sort of plan. I always knew, though, that I wouldn't marry.

If I never married, I'd never divorce. I'd be safe, exempt from my family's legacy of divorce.

WHEN WOMEN COMPLAIN ABOUT THEIR MOTHERS, THEY most often say that they are too controlling, too critical, and too interested in keeping a paw on all the minor decisions of their grown daughters' lives. This stereotypical mother has something to say about every decision her daughter makes—from the cut of her slacks to her choice of apples for pies. This mother knows the minutiae of her daughter's life, no matter how advanced in age the daughter may be or how far away from her mother she may live, and this mother seems to be everywhere—in the movies, on the sidelines of beauty contests, in the changing room of Ann Taylor—with an endless stream of comments on the subject of how her daughter should live.

This is not my mother. My mother has not tried to control the small details of my life. Most of the small details of my life are, frankly, of no interest to her. She has always had a large hazy affection for the whole of me, but very little interest in the happenings of my day. As a child, I never heard direct criticism from my mother, but I never heard any truly specific praise, either. She sometimes forgot the names of my teachers and friends and whether I was taking French that semester. While I was relieved not to be under the scrutiny that some of my friends received from their mothers, I often felt like I had slipped a little too successfully under her radar. I could do just about anything and my mom would smile and say what a good girl I was, because she so didn't want to deal with anything but a good girl.

And so I was good. Mostly. And when I wasn't, it went unnoticed. I was also really, really pissed off—not in the kind of way where you know you are pissed off, but in the kind of way where you gain thirty pounds and you don't know why. Eventually I had a daughter of my own, and I suddenly knew exactly why I sometimes ground my molars down to a fine powder when my mom was around.

It started three weeks after Natalie was born. My mother came to visit, and I mistakenly thought she was there, like your typical grandmother, to help. This was not the case. From what I could tell this visit was no different to her from visits that had taken place during the pre-baby era, which meant that she expected to read the paper, golf, and linger over a few martinis before dinner. It also meant she did not notice that her daughter was insanely exhausted and had fallen prostrate with postpartum depression onto the subur-ban shag carpeting.

My mother would hold Natalie for seven and a half min-utes and then say, "Okay, back to Mama," just when I was starting to nod off on the couch. She kept insisting that Natalie could "cry it out" in the crib even though I showed her every scrap of baby literature I had, all of which insisted that parents should *always* go to a crying baby, and that it was impossible to spoil an infant. And she told a story about a black housekeeper who held a baby on her hip with one arm and stirred soup with the other, all the while calling out orders to her other children in a happy singsong voice. (Somehow, in my mother's telling, the race of the woman was important, as if she were saying that if I were black and maybe a housekeeper, then perhaps I could be more at ease with the role of motherhood.)

I was not saying anything in a happy singsong sort of voice. I was mumbling under my breath and kicking doors open with my feet. I was rushing over to the calendar to count the days until she left. I was hating myself for being an incompetent mother *and* a hateful daughter. When she was finally gone, I redoubled my efforts to be a mother who was never frazzled or bored by motherhood. But my resolve was in vain because I was still frazzled and in me there would always be at least a little bit of my detached mother.

She might not have been the most stellar example of nurturing motherhood, but my mom was the sort of woman who could make divorce look good. She carried a tan leather suitcase, drove a bright blue convertible, and kept her wavy hair blond and short. Divorced for the second time in 1962, she was out of step with the married women around her—including my friends' mothers, who mesmerized me with their cake-decorating skills and their well-regulated homes. A successful businesswoman accustomed to working in a man's world, she mingled with the other mothers in her pencil skirts and sling-back high heels as if she were a movie star—more prone to tumultuous relationships, sure, but also exempt from the Donna Reed–style expectations that still hemmed in the lives of many women. Part of her financial success stemmed from the fact that the construction business she and my father had started up together was the right thing at the right time. California was growing, and housing prices were on the rise.

She was a woman who loved men and all things masculine. She delighted in cold, dry martinis in smoky, mahogany bars, stock market tips, medium-rare T-bones, men who resembled Clark Gable, and anchoring down at the yacht club. She liked the business world and has prospered in it. But there was another card my mother carried in her pocket, one that I wouldn't fully understand the power of until I was a grown woman myself.

My mother had a boyfriend. He was good looking. He was rich. And he was married. He would never leave his wife, but his devotion to my mother would never fade. She was perpetually loved and perpetually safe from dreary domesticity. She was set. Or just about.

WHEN NATALIE WAS A TODDLER, I WENT TO CALIFORNIA by myself to see my paternal grandmother, JoJo. It was late summer, and we sat on her deck in the shade of the huge apricot tree that had yielded jam for three generations, the sweet sticky stuff we'd heaped on toast and on vanilla ice cream as children. We talked a little about my new life as a mother, but she was clearly bored by chatter about baby's first steps and baby's first haircut. JoJo was smart and well read. She had xeriscaped before most anyone else in California and watched the *McNeil-Lehrer News Hour* in the evenings and abhorred network news watchers who let their automatic sprinklers shower the state's dwindling water supply onto their chemically fertilized lawns. I always wanted her to think we were on the same side, the thinking person's side. Maybe she'd be happier, I thought, if we talked about the past. I remembered the dreamy look she always got when she spoke about her days at Mills College, across the bay. She said "Mills" with a sigh, as if it were another word for heaven.

"So, what was my mother like when I was a baby?" I asked.

"Your mother," she said coolly, "saw herself as something of a sexpot back then."

I remembered that expression from my childhood. Marilyn Monroe was a sexpot, and so was Betty Grable. But no one's *mother* was called a sexpot. And the only thing less dignified than being a sexpot, it seemed to me, was seeing yourself as something of one. I flashed on a photo of my mother that she'd stuck to the fridge with a magnet around the time I was busy gaining my teenage heft. It was a picture of her as a very young woman with her blond hair curled Veronica Lake style, her head bowed, her eyes cast up doe-style at the camera. Her shirt was tied in a knot at her midriff, accentuating her breasts and her slender waist. The gay boy I had a crush on in the twelfth grade plucked the photo off the fridge, exhaled a wolf whistle, and asked in his large theater voice, "Who is *this*?" I supposed she had put the picture up as an incentive to stick to her diet, but to me it felt like a constant reminder of all the beauty and power my mom possessed and all I was sure I would not.

"And she sure knew how to get rid of her kids. She was always dropping them off here, there, everywhere," JoJo said, poking her Pall Mall 100 in the air to indicate the diverse locations of "here, there, everywhere."

Shame burned through me. Somehow I felt guilty *for* my mom. I was tempted to defend her to my grandmother. But then a recent memory of my mother shuddered through me, a scene that confirmed that what my grandmother was saying was true, and there was no point trying to say it wasn't.

Like many of the moments of my complicated feelings toward her, this one involved an act of generosity on my mother's part. My mother will always have more money than I do. It's a metaphysical thing. While my money drains like water from checking and money-market accounts, hers multiplies and multiplies. I imagine bank accounts overflowing with white furry rabbits, their numbers increasing exponentially, crowding one another with soft ears flopping until they overflow into bonds and S&P 500 funds, a few rabbits skimmed off now and then for a trip to Palm Desert or a generous donation to the good people of Amnesty International or Planned Parenthood. As much as I want to say, "I care not for your money and what it can buy," my heart betrays me, leaping at the sight of her folded checks in envelopes stuffed full of clippings of articles on the plummeting of Lucent stock, shares of which—we both recall—I bought just before the price crested and crashed.

The setting for this hand-that-feeds-me scene was Nordstrom's, a place I probably wouldn't shop when spending my own money. But that day I wasn't spending my own money. I had flown with my breast-feeding baby, Natalie, to my mother's city for an interview for a job I desperately wanted. My mother was going to buy me a suit for the interview. I was accomplished enough to have jobs that required suits, or at least a suit for the interview, but not powerful enough to buy them on my own.

Natalie was a baby who fared best with a lot of action, so this day of rushing through airports and stores had kept her satisfied. Now she sat back in the stroller contentedly, her big dark eyes roaming around. Meanwhile, my mother and I sifted through racks and racks of gray and black and blue. But another metaphysical law was in operation that day: The amount of money available to buy a thing is always in direct opposition to that thing's availability. We were having no luck. I was getting tired, and as much as I wanted the free suit, I was losing interest in looking. I decided to give it one last try. Pushing onward, into a department too dense with racks of clothes to accommodate a stroller, I asked my mother if she would watch Natalie for a few minutes. "Sure," she said.

How long had I looked at silky blouses and suits of padded shoulders when it happened? Five minutes, maybe? I looked up from a rounder of blouses, and there she was, a few feet away, browsing without a care, stopping and then dismissing each hanger with a little push. She was alone. *Alone*.

"Mom!"

"What, dear?"

"Mo-o-om! Where's *Nat*-a-lie?"

"Oh, honey, she's over there, near the escalators." She waved in the direction we had come from, toward the urban, kidnapper-crowded escalators.

I couldn't see the stroller. I ran and I ran. Illogically, I started shouting her name: Natalie, *Natalie*! In this tasteful setting, with the store pianist tinkling something from Cole Porter, I was a frothing, shouting madwoman whose child had fallen into the hands of wolves. How far did I run through racks of clothing, past slow-moving ladies in their summer dresses? Sixty feet, maybe? And there she was, happy in her fuzzy purple sweater, her stroller parked in a cluster of soft chairs about ten feet from the top of the up escalator. She smiled at me. She was fine, but I was not. I had been left alone and helpless. I was a baby in the care of a distracted woman. I unclipped her straps and lifted her to my heart. She felt so warm and smelled so good, her presence pure comfort. Hush now. Mama's here. It's all over. I'll never let you out of my sight again. I won't think about me or my suit. All I want is you, you, you.

My mom ambled over with a pair of white shorts in her hand. "I'm going to go try these on."

She didn't know! She didn't even know that she'd done anything wrong. How could she not know? Couldn't she see my rage? Surely I'd been transformed. Didn't I look like that Human Torch character from the Fantastic Four—the one who would shout "Flame on!" and turn into a human form of fire?

"You were shopping for shorts!" I clutched Natalie to me as if I'd just pulled her out of a fire.

"I know. The last thing I need is another pair of white shorts," she laughed.

"You said you would watch her while I shopped."

"I *was* watching her," she said, her tone finally growing defensive.

"You were over there and she was here. How could you have been watching her?"

"She was fine."

"So which is it? You were watching her? Or you weren't, but you think she was okay anyway?"

"Dear, there's no problem. She's fine." She gave me The Look.

I'd seen The Look plenty in the last nine months. The Look could be decoded as, You sure are a tightly strung new mother, aren't you? The truth is, most times when she gave me The Look I probably deserved it. I *was* a tightly strung new mother. I was disproportionately nutty and tense. Only a few weeks earlier I'd seen a story on *Oprah* about a child

who'd stood in her crib to look out the window and stran-
gled herself on a blind cord. My Natalie couldn't even roll
over yet but no matter. Off the cords went.

But this was different. This wasn't me being crazy. My
mother had left the person I loved most in an unsafe place.
The worst part was she wasn't sorry. She didn't even think
she'd done anything wrong! In fact, in her mind, I was the
one with the problem. I was, once again, the hysteric.

My psyche had turned into a cubist painting. I was the
baby who was left. I could feel the silence that always followed my mother's retreat from me. I was also the daughter
who'd asked her mother for help and had been let down. But
I knew, too, that part of me was also the woman unaccount-
able, the rogue spirit who could leave or betray others, the
one who could twist things to see all my actions as harmless.
I'd seen in the last nine months that parenthood hadn't dis-
solved my restlessness, this family legacy of desire. I, too,
had ambitions that could blind me to my daughter and her
needs. But a pair of white shorts just wasn't one of them.

"It's not 1957, you know. There are weirdos everywhere," I said, gesturing toward the two Tipper Gore looka-
likes ringing up their purchases at the nearby register. "And
they'd love to take a nice baby like this."

"You sit down here," she said, guiding me into one of the
easy chairs as though I were recovering from surgery. "I'm
going to try on these shorts." She took a few steps toward
the fitting rooms, and then turned back, thinking, I suppose,
that she'd offer some motherly guidance.

"There is nothing wrong," she said firmly. And then she glided off to the fitting rooms with her white shorts.

MOTHERHOOD BROUGHT WITH IT A VULNERABILITY I'D avoided most of my life. After I became a mother, I *needed* people—people who would watch my daughter when I had strep throat, who'd assure me that the sleep deprivation would end or teach me how to rein in a defiant toddler. Sometimes that need gave me a chance to trust, and sometimes it ushered in disappointment. Mostly, I haven't trusted. I've taken on more than I could handle, rather than ask for help. In eighth-grade drama class, we all took turns falling backward into the group's outstretched arms. I was the one who couldn't do it. Try as I might, I couldn't let go. I couldn't let those hands break my fall.

Divorce has made me feel even more vulnerable. As a single mom, I'm now one person doing the two-person job of earning a living and caring for kids. And even though all sorts of other people do this, I know now that they are doing the impossible, or at least the impossible for me. I can't sacrifice sleep, peace of mind, and all hope of leisure. I'm not heroic or even particularly energetic. So I'm going to have to ask my mom, my friends, relatives, and even acquaintances for help, and I'll have to fall back into their outstretched hands.

But I still want to be seen as the helper, not the helpee. I fear the *no* that carries the sting of rejection even if it wasn't intended as that. I fear putting people on the spot. But mostly I fear that my friends and family will perceive me as I truly am—a broke, beleaguered, needy, and generally desperate single mother who's on the verge of a nervous breakdown. (What, by the way, *is* a nervous breakdown? Why don't people seem to have them anymore? In the fifties it seemed a woman in my position would be a strong candidate for a nervous breakdown. When I was growing up, I overheard my mother speaking quietly about a woman who "had a breakdown." But this option is not open to me because I don't know what one looks like, or how to tell if I'm having one.)

It looks as though I'm either going to have to learn to bend time and space or I'm going to have to trust that I will receive the help I need. Somehow defying the laws of physics seems the easier answer. But I know that if I don't learn to ask for help, I'll feel so alone and overburdened that I'll take my frustration out on the kids.

The night Kevin left, I called my friend Anika at home and on her cell. I wasn't sure what message to leave. I just asked her to call me, no matter how late. She called at ten. She'd just received the message. When I told her Kevin had left and I was sure it was for good, she asked me if I wanted her to come over.

"But it's so late, and don't you have to drive over to work in the morning?" I was surprised that she would come over on a weeknight. The commute from my house to her office could be as long as an hour. It was too much to ask for her to do that.

"But this is really important. You don't want to be there alone, do you?"

I shook my head into the phone. A big knot was in my throat, making it impossible to speak. I realized in a rush just how profoundly I did not want to be alone. And yet it hadn't occurred to me to ask my closest friend to come to me in what was clearly one of my darkest hours.

An hour later she was at my house with her next day's clothes on a hanger and a small overnight bag. She stayed a week, sleeping beside me in the king-size bed in the spot that had been my husband's. Some nights Jessie would crawl in between us and snuggle into the spot she had always claimed as her own, the one she called "the middle," a place soon to exist only in the historical sense, like Yugoslavia or the Ottoman Empire.

During the day, I'd call Anika at work and ask her what she wanted for dinner. In the afternoons before I picked up the kids from school, I shopped in a wifely way for the vegetarian foods I hoped she would like. A couple of nights we ate French pastries from the bakery and drank red wine in bed with the TV on in the background, talking over the shows and during the commercials like a married couple, or maybe better, like very good friends. When I woke up panicked in the middle of the night, I gently shook her shoulder and said, "Anika, I'm really, really scared," and she listened to me until I was finally ready to go back to sleep. It was a beautiful respite from all the heinous adult activities of my days—calling the lawyer, talking to the girls' teachers, breathing. For a few hours each day, I was cared for in just the way I needed, as though I were the girl and she were my mother.

3

Hunt, Gather, and File for Legal Separation

I used to think *single mother* was the scariest phrase in the English language, but a few days ago I realized there's worse and that *embittered wife* must surely top the list of people I did not want to become. So I'm hoping to do this thing called "the good divorce," in which separated parents speak civilly when escorting the children to each other's homes and find consensus on such volatile topics as sugar consumption and the minimum age for ear piercing. Essentially, I'm attempting in my divorce to do the same thing I kept hoping to do with my marriage: fly over the low bar my parents set forty-some years ago.

But I'm not sure I'm going to have the sanity to pull such a thing off. It takes a certain sangfroid to keep a divorce "good," to put your anger and frustration aside and let the higher good of the children, of the family, fragmented as it is now, be the beacon that guides you. Chief among my irritants is money and the fact that our family income has moved into an apartment around the corner. At the moment all I can rely upon is child support and a meager "maintenance" check, which means that our adjusted annual income will hover near the poverty line. Sometimes I can't believe I got myself into this vulnerable position, but it doesn't take much—an unpaid doctor's bill, a stray thought about all the money Kevin wasted and what it could've done for our family—for disbelief to morph into rage.

When Natalie was two, I began inching away from work and toward stay-at-home motherhood. There was no single dramatic moment when I gave up my career for the domestic life, just a series of small choices—first to take a sabbatical from my position as a full-time professor, then to teach part-time instead of returning to the community college, and then finally to allow part-time work to fade into occasional contract work that was little more than a hobby. At the same time, Kevin's income was increasing. He left social work for real estate at a time when the Seattle housing market was moving from warm to hot.

And so all four of us came to expect and depend on my presence at home. I'd once been scared to be "just a mom," and although I was still nervous about moving too far away from the world of adults, intelligent conversation, and clean clothing, I found a joy in my new life: I volunteered at the preschool co-op, drove the girls to parks and lessons and museums, and hosted playdates, sleepovers, and tea parties. This new version of myself kept tiny boxes of raisins in her purse and ate peanut butter sandwiches at the park with her new mom friends.

But for a stay-at-home mom, divorce isn't just divorce. It's more like divorce plus losing your job. The job I once had—stay-at-home-mom-slash-dilettante-writer—no longer exists. When I worked at the community college, we called women in my position "displaced homemakers." Now I imagine legions of these red-gingham-aproned Betty Crockers spinning out into the outer edges of the atmosphere, perpetually tracing their feather dusters across imaginary furniture, never ceasing to "make" the "home" that is no longer there.

I add up our expenses for a month and subtract Kevin's contribution from the total. The number indicates that to stay out of debt, I will need to net annually one-third more than I've ever made in my life. My children boast to their friends that their mom is a writer and professor, and while this is intermittently true, neither of those occupations in their current incarnations generates an annual income larger than that of a collegiate salesgirl at FAO Schwarz.

IT'S FIVE DAYS AFTER THE SPLIT, AND I AM WAITING TO meet with my attorney—the Divorce King of Seattle, from what I can tell—to discuss the parenting plan, child support, and how the bounty of my marriage is to be divided. He told me on the phone to bring the piece of paper that scares me the most: our credit report. So now I'm sitting here in the waiting room, trying to work up the nerve to open the envelope. Terrified of my reaction, Kevin has so far refused to tell me—he probably doesn't know himself—how much he secretly gambled away over the last year and a half. My hope is that it's less than ten thousand dollars; my fear is that it's closer to a hundred thousand, a number that undoubtedly would mean losing our house.

The taupe-colored sofas in this room are packed with women in their forties and fifties awaiting their fates, all looking extremely worried and what my mother calls "drawn." One forty-fiveish woman with a box of legal papers balanced on her lap has only a thin veneer of hair, combed neatly over the curve of her delicate skull. I consider for a moment two things: the possibility that I look as bad as these women do, and that there's some reason—one that no one will admit but that I may soon discover—why it's only women who fill this room.

I look at the time. Two minutes until my 11:00 a.m. appointment. I tell myself to do it quickly, like taking off a Band-Aid. And finally I open the credit report. Names of credit cards pop off the page. Chase Manhattan and Bank of America are the first two I see. I scan the list with my heartbeat thrumming in my ears and dare to count: in addition to the two credit cards I know about, there are seven more I had no idea existed. Legally, I could be held responsible for these debts, even though I knew nothing about them until today. I pencil the numbers in the margin and add them up: the total is roughly the equivalent of a year's tuition at an Ivy

League university. I blink and blink again, trying to process the information. But I can't.

It's as though I'm downloading into my brain some graphics-heavy file that keeps the hourglass running and bars access to any other programs. The primary mental task of this day will be to reconcile myself to the disparity between my image of my life and my actual life. I've been duped by the person I trusted most, and there's some chance that the signs had been there for me to observe all along and that I chose not to see them.

The receptionist calls my name, and I go in to see the attorney.

For the next four hours we map out Natalie's and Jess's weekly and annual schedules. "Before you can get a legal separation, every moment of their lives must be accounted for on paper," the lawyer tells me when I start to whine and pose lackadaisical questions like, "Can't we just see how it goes?" Oddly, there's a software program with drop-down menus for creating parenting plans—another reminder of just how many of us are busy figuring out how to extricate ourselves from tightly entwined lives. So all afternoon the attorney fires questions at me, such as, "Do you want the children picked up from school by their father on Wednesdays or Tuesdays?" "Do you want to have Christmas with the girls on odd or even years? Do you want to split Christmas Day and have a switch time at noon? Or switch on the twenty-sixth?" "Presidents' Day, any preference?" I find myself flippantly making choices: yes, odd years, noon on Saturdays, and hold the mayo. But then I remember that these are our lives, and the process becomes tediously slow as I mull over the ramifications of every decision.

Tomorrow, we'll move on to child support. It turns out there's a formula for calculating the support payments, involving the income of both parents and the percentage of time the children spend with each of them. Of course, this makes perfect sense—these decisions can't be made from scratch by each new divorcing couple—but still I'm terrified by how clinical it all is, by how easily one's life can be reduced to a number.

As I'm gathering my papers to leave, the attorney says, "Just bring in copies of all your tax returns tomorrow, with the W-2s, bank statements from the last year, and, oh, all your credit card statements as well." He says this in a casual tone that suggests that locating these documents is a task that others consider not only possible but straightforward.

It occurs to me now, perched before his enormous, pristine desk, that I am not organized enough to get a divorce. Other people have file cabinets. I have a crawlspace stuffed with dripping pads of ripped insulation and boxes of books and old papers. I try to visualize the remote box in the crawlspace that might contain all our returns, but I can't. I ask him whether I can use his phone to call our accountant, Janet.

Janet is a mother from Natalie's Brownie troop. Like everyone in Seattle (or so it seems now in my divorce-induced paranoia), she's part of a two-parent, skiing-on-the-weekends family, and I dread filling her in on the situation. When she answers, the words rush out of me: "Hi-Janet-how-are-you-I'm-getting-a-legal-separation-this-week-can-I-have-copies-of-the-last-four-years'-returns? Today?" Janet tells me how sorry she is in a kind and gentle way that makes me want to weep inconsolably, and then offers to drive over with the returns.

"But I'm not at home," I say sheepishly, looking out beyond the plate-glass windows of the attorney's downtown office at the panoramic view of a royal blue Puget Sound and the jagged line of the Olympic Mountains.

"That's okay, I'll drop them off at your house," she offers.

I'm silent for a minute as I imagine my precious returns—packed with social security numbers, stapled-on W-2s, gross incomes and adjusted incomes—exposed on my front porch. "Don't worry," she says, as though reading my thoughts. "I'll put them on the back porch, underneath the mat."

A picture of my back porch flashes into my mind. First of all, there is no mat. There is, however, a garbage pail full of various hair gels and shampoos, left there last summer when my then-husband decided to "clean" the bathroom, and a heap of wet, filthy tea towels, cast out the kitchen door to await the next load of hot-water wash. There's also a jumble of cardboard boxes full of various items—mangled coloring books, children's underwear, to name a few—I pulled out of my car in a number of halfhearted attempts to finally clean it.

"Oh, thanks. That's really nice," I say, all the while thinking: This is it. This is divorce. When you're married, your hatches are safely battened. All your failings and trash can be kept nicely out of sight. But divorce is more like: Here I am, world! Me and my dirty porch, come and see!

IN MY CIRCLE OF GOOD FRIENDS, THERE ARE THREE women I've known since childhood. Coincidentally, all four of us married in 1992 and 1993, when we were teetering around our thirtieth birthdays. Two of my friends are still married; their combined marriages, which have outlasted infertility, a run-in with cancer, deteriorating parents, and a season-long separation, are sometimes strained, perhaps, but still intact. The other two marriages—Nancy's and mine—have now ended.

Nancy's wedding took place on a spring afternoon on a bluff overlooking a vivid stretch of British Columbia's shoreline. Partway through the ceremony, the minister broke his attention from the couple before him and spoke to the guests in a commanding voice: "It is up to the community to hold a couple together. Each of you here, witnesses to this event, are responsible for remembering for this couple the love that brought them together and the commitment they've made." One year into my own happy marriage then, I took his words to heart, vowing to myself to support Nancy and Terry, to remind Nancy of Terry's strengths if someday she came to me to vent after a marital spat. Yet despite their vows and ours, Nancy and Terry, ten years and two sons later, couldn't be held together any longer. And neither could we.

Each of these women I grew up with has a tangible skill, something she does with her hands that people need and want, a trade that exists outside the realm of childhood fantasy careers like astronaut or movie star. One is an electrician, another a graphic artist, the third a nurse. Inside or outside of marriage, they can support themselves. Nancy, the electrician, tools around town still in the same red van she drove when she was married—the one with the yellow electric bolt on the side panel advertising NANCY'S ELECTRICAL SERVICE. My own skill, however, is to a career as buying lotto tickets is to investing. Like the child who proudly lists "President of the United States" as his future vocation, I stubbornly insist that I am a writer. For the last three years I've been writing a memoir about a happily married woman and her transition into motherhood. *Light Sleeper: The Making of an Unlikely Mother,* it's called. The only trouble is, my agent can't find a publisher that wants to buy it. And, oh, I'm not happily married anymore. But other than that . . .

One of my writer friends, Christina, sells short, upbeat pieces about her life and reads them aloud on NPR. She lives in California, a lot closer to the pulse than I am here in Seattle, but she convinces me that I, too, could be churning my life into radio stories. Okay, I think, I can do that! I start to brainstorm ideas. What about the holidays? I can write short, upbeat pieces about being a single mom for the first time during the holidays. I won't actually need to get a *real* job! I'll write a few pieces, NPR will buy them, then they'll buy a few more, and then one day I'll wake up to realize I've morphed into a female David Sedaris. I test-drive a few ideas—the heady confusion of pulling together your first Thanksgiving dinner on your own, deciding what to do about Christmas cards (truncated family photo, or no photo at all?), Christmas shopping without a mate, managing all those bags and parcels solo. Or maybe I could talk about what it's like to feel yourself swirling within the ever-tightening tornado of pre-Christmas hysteria alone while the kids' heads are still spinning from the news of the divorce?

It takes me only a few minutes to realize there is nothing upbeat about this. I can't possibly arrive at "okay" in the two minutes a radio piece allows the narrator to travel from universal-but-not-devastating problem to complicated-but-hopeful resignation.

Yet I still fantasize that my career or "love life" might suddenly manifest some sign of impending victory. Perhaps a seemingly random sequence of events will lead to my lucrative dream job. Perhaps I will meet and marry an amazing man who adores my daughters and makes me realize that the good love I felt for Husband #1 was just a prelude. But as ordinary non-triumphant day follows ordinary non-triumphant day, it occurs to me that the climactic scene in which my hopes are realized might never happen. My life, after all, is not *Bend It Like Beckham*.

After a month of non-triumphant days has passed, the school Halloween carnival arrives. There's nothing like dressing up in something festive when your heart is swollen in pain and your legs are wooden with confusion about where to step next. Determined to prove that I'm still a fun mother, I decide I must wear a costume this year, even though in the past I've shown up in jeans and a sweatshirt. I have no more parenting laurels to rest on. I go to the store and search for the cheapest and least invasive costume I can find. I settle on a pair of green monarch butterfly wings and matching antennae—two fluorescent green pom-poms waving insanely at the end of their springs. The symbolism—the costume's cheery insistence that there is life after the cocoon—is not lost on me. I wear the wings with a heart full of irony.

After the carnival, we gather outside, where Natalie and her friend Ellen are recounting the plot of an inane preteen movie they saw on cable last night. I do not have cable, but Natalie's dad has it at his new apartment. She has entered the Kingdom of the Privileged, and this is part of her excitement with Ellen. She has at once become a part of a special world her friend inhabits—the illicit cable culture her mother scorns—and a citizen of the nation of broken families, a country still invisible to nine-year-old Ellen. After they've reenacted the movie in its entirety, Natalie adds, "I watched it at my dad's house." Ellen's father, who's clearly hearing the news for the first time, looks up and his eyes meet mine until finally I look down. The single one, I'm learning, is like the new dog at the kennel: always the one to look away first.

One of the many things I'll have to learn in the coming months is how to break this news to the world, or at least to that sliver of the world that cares. One of the divorce books heaped about on the floor beside my bed urges me to develop two stories about the divorce: a private one and a public one. I should rehearse a few sentences I can recite—in the grocery store or the school foyer—without excessive emotion, a sort of campaign slogan for the divorce that cuts short the whys and the hows that need not be explored in random social encounters with tertiary associates. The private story should not, the book advises, be the same as the public one and need not be interchangeable with my ex's version of the events that led to the termination of our marriage, but rather should be my own personal narrative that creates order out of my undifferentiated chaos.

In some ways the book's advice makes sense, as it does seem like much of each day's work now is negotiating the icy pass that traverses the gap between my private and public selves. Alone, I shriek into my pillow and shout "bonehead" through my closed car windows as I drive past my ex's apartment building. In public, I'm stoic, detached, nodding philosophically as a married mother from Natalie's soccer team tells me and a cluster of other married women that my "grief is like a house." "One day," she tells me, "you'll be in the room of sorrow and the next you might be in anger." The humbled divorcée, I can only nod as if all this were news to me.

"And oh, denial!" she adds. "That's a room, too, don't forget."

I'm starting to think of going out of the house as "coming out," since it inevitably means running into people I know, but not so well that they *know,* and each of these meetings shaves a few years off my life. If I were to tell all the casual friends I run into what's going on, it would be awkward for them and excruciating for me, but when I don't, it feels as though everything I say is a lie. Certainly it's a lie to tell them everything's "fine," but it even feels like a falsehood to talk about ordinary life——Natalie's soccer team, Jess's new penchant for scootering. Any subject other than the breakup of my marriage feels like lying by omission. There seems to be only one honest sentence I can speak: "I'm getting divorced." Everything else plays at the tinny frequency of rehearsed speech, like the spiel that flight attendants give about what to do in the event of a drop in cabin pressure.

But I have no idea how to tell people or whether it's even necessary for me to tell them at all. I feel like I'm completely off-road, beyond the bounds of normal human communication, freewheeling it. Yet *lots* of people divorce. How do they handle it? Surely there's a way, but I don't have the strength or stamina to figure it out right now.

This morning in the grocery store I saw from afar a woman I knew from the preschool co-op. She's a dancer who taught Natalie and the other preschoolers to reach up, up, up like flowers yearning for the sun and droop down, down, down like tired rag dolls. Even pushing a cart through a grocery store, she has great posture (no slumping over the handle) and glides gracefully past the pyramids of oranges and apples. I found myself scooting from aisle to aisle to avoid her, keeping my head nearly in the cart as if I were concentrating on something serious and important there. (What? The label on the soy-milk carton?) Despite my maneuvering, we arrived at the checkout lanes at the same time, but somehow I still managed to dodge direct eye contact, and I left the store relieved, as though I'd just freed myself from some horrible peril.

But while I was driving home, I realized I hadn't escaped as cleanly as I thought. I'd detoured around the social moment, but I'd missed the chance to get outside of myself, if only for a short time. I'm the type of person who adores running into an old acquaintance. I would have loved to hear how her three kids were doing in school and sports, and even if I'd broken down and wept in front of the frozen pizzas, I think this woman would have treated me with kindness. She might have felt sad for me, but she wouldn't have judged me. It was *me* who judged me.

Even though I'm not yet ready to look old acquaintances in the eye and tell it like it is, I am—apparently—ready to come out, Tourette's-style, to random strangers: baristas, store clerks, door-to-door campaigners for human rights. In the last few weeks I've held—to my surprise as much as theirs—a few innocents captive for a moment to divulge confidential material even some of my friends don't know.

"I'd love to give money to your organization, but I'm getting divorced, and honestly I don't know how I'm going to make it financially as it is. Sure, there's money in the house, but it's not like you can pay the dentist with that. I guess you could say it's not really a good time," I said to the eighteen-year-old human rights advocate who clutched his clipboard a little tighter and stared at the doormat, saying, "Oh, I'm sorry." I felt both guilty and strange as I closed the door, just as I had when the girl making my Americano casually asked what I was up to on such a beautiful day and I told her that I was off to my attorney's to draft my legal separation agreement. I guess I was checking to see if the world would split in two if I spoke these truths out loud. But of course, no matter what I say or don't say, the world remains intact. It is pretty much just my world that has been torn down the middle. Or at least that's how it feels.

Eventually I will have to tell everyone who hasn't heard through the grapevine. Some people will get the whole story and some people will just get a terse "We've separated" without explanation. The trick is deciding who gets what. The whole-story people are exhausting. At first it's a relief, and I'm all adrenaline as I recount the seconds in which I knew the shuttle was breaking apart. But then I'm filled with dread as I realize there are still legions of people who deserve and need to hear the whole story. Still ahead of me are dozens of oh-my-Gods and oh-I'm-so-sorrys and you-must-be-kiddings. I can hear the sympathetic and under-standable questions coming at me one after another, and I can feel my tongue, thick and unfamiliar, forming all these tedious words one more time.

I consider a form letter that begins,

Dear Good Friend Who Deserves the Whole Story,
> I'm sorry this is coming to you as a form letter.
> I'm sorry about a lot.
> I'm just sorry.

Or maybe I could build a website, www.whatthe#&?!happened.com, complete with an FAQ page:

Q. What about the children?
A. They live with me but they will stay with him every
   Friday and every first, third, and fifth Thursday night,
   as well as the first Saturday of every month. Yes, it
   is hard to remember which week it is. Yes, at least
   once a day the children mention the movie *The Parent
   Trap,* in which a pair of ingenious, separated-at-birth-
   but-reunited-by-fate twins scheme until their divorced
   parents finally and joyously reconcile. Which brings
   us to the next inevitable question . . .
Q. Will reconciliation be possible?
A. No. If you read The Whole Story (use password to

access the secure site), you will shake your head and
say, "No, you cannot get back together." If you do not
have access to The Whole Story, you—like the Trans-
portation Coordinator at my younger daughter's
school—may feel compelled to advise me to go back
and try to work it out and say in a scornful voice
what a shame it is when families break up.

Q. Are you okay?

A. No, I'm not. Thanks for asking.

Q. Is there anything we can do to help?

A. Yes, click on the "Send Money" link below. Most
major credit cards accepted.

WHEN I TAKE OFF MY WEDDING RINGS, MY FINGER LOOKS
pale and atrophied underneath, which seems almost exces-
sively symbolic. I protect the white band of skin with my
thumb, as though it were a wound. I stare at other women's
ring fingers—gold bands, simple solitaires, swirling clusters
of diamonds. The fact that they've managed to keep those
rings on seems as miraculous as a defiance of gravity. When I
wore my wedding rings, I was a different person, emboldened the way you can be in a Halloween costume. I could
laugh as loud as I wanted and go out with dirty hair and
sweatpants. I was married! I belonged. Someone loved me
and it showed. I could reference a husband to a new friend
or a store clerk. They didn't care if I was married or not, but

I did. My ring said, You can't touch me. It was like base in a game of tag. I was safe.

I turn the electric blanket on high when I go to bed. I lie there soaking up the heat like a nutrient. Sometimes I think of this divorce business as something like a flu. The feverish beginnings, miserable and sweaty as they are, are somehow easier to get through—they blur by, really—than the many half-well, half-sick days that follow, days when you're not sure what to do. You're too well to stay in bed watching TV, but too sick to go out and do all the things well people are expected to do. Too sad to carry young by the nape of the neck or to think of mating again.

To fall asleep, I fall back on my old routine of counting my blessings. I count my two daughters over and over again. I count their health, their happiness, the gift of who they are. And right before I fall asleep, I add one more item to the list: the knowledge that I can no longer live under the magical spell of married, middle-class thinking. I'm not the woman who can pretend everything's working out just great anymore. I know that it's up to me now to hunt, to gather, and to keep shelter warm.

4

After the Eclipse

My sister and I lie feet-to-feet in a hammock strung between palms that sway together like a postcard cliché. Thirty miles west of here, on the other side of the Baja's fingertip of land, the sun is dunking into the Pacific. Kathy and I sip tequila from plastic cups as the Sea of Cortez, fading now to a washed-out indigo, laps gently onto our strip of sand.

Kathy and my mother thought a vacation might be just the rest cure I need, and I couldn't agree more. I feel a bit shaky and British in this role of fragile, indebted divorcée, though—something like the perennial E. M. Forster character who's subject to swooning and poor judgment, the one perpetually being shipped off to the Continent by her wealthy London relatives after some unspeakable incident involving yet another bounder.

It's starting to sink in that I've done the thing I was sure I could not—would not—do. Like my mother before me and my two grandmothers before her, I have left my husband. I spent a lot of my grown-up life trying to dodge their fate, and now, like a character in a Greek tragedy, I find that all my efforts to avoid this end have done nothing but slam me headlong into it. Throughout my adolescence and my twenties, I swore that I would never marry. And when I finally did, I hoped I might have an edge on fate because I'd waited until I was thirty and my education was finished. My daughters were both born into a two-parent home, and a pretty happy one at that. I was sure I could shield them from some of the uncertainty and longing that had haunted me throughout my childhood, that I could give them the seamless family I had always wanted myself, one with a mother and father in the same house and on the same side.

I already knew from experience that for children divorce means half the world is constantly eclipsed. When you're with one parent, the other must always slip out of view. I knew, too, how a yearning for home could become a part of you much too young, and unless you were very lucky or strong or some combination of the two, you could spend most of your life searching for that feeling of wholeness that once eluded you, for that ordered kingdom that disappeared before you could ever come into your own and leave it for a world of your own making.

I knew this. I knew it all, and still I left.

AMERICANS LINE THE STREET HERE IN SAN JOSÉ DEL Cabo, trying in vain to find the taxi stop rumored to be somewhere along this crooked half-mile of shops. A teenager is cursing his stepfather's inability to hail a cab. His mother shrugs and forces a weak smile that says, *My life has spiraled so far out of my control that I'm no longer even going to try*. The stepfather—increasingly desperate to prove himself—swings his arms wildly as yet another cab whizzes by. Behind them the noise of the street fair rises—yelps from plummeting rides, eighties pop music scratching from loudspeakers.

This American family, like my sister and me, probably wandered aimlessly for the last hour around the hot and dusty streets of the fair, gawking at the pink hunk of meat rolling on a rotisserie, buying packets of miniature Chiclets— infatuated, no doubt, with the novelty of their smallness. But this fair is for the people of San José. It is not for us; we are uninvited guests. We are tolerated for our dollars, but we are not loved, and so like anyone tolerated but not loved, we eventually yearn for home, even if home for now is just the comfort of a familiar hotel room frosty with air-conditioning.

I'm pretty sure, though, that we won't make it back to the resort for a long time. Besides this family, there is a sun-burned Midwestern couple who are clearly ahead of us in this endless wait for a cab. The large, doughy husband leaning into his cane looks to me like he's both diabetic and on the verge of heatstroke.

My sister wanders over to a young Mexican waiter at an outdoor café. He is twenty, with slicked-back black hair and a crisp white shirt, and even though my sister is clearly a *señora*—albeit a blond and beautiful one—there is some-

thing flirtatious in their interaction. Even if I could hear
them from here at the curb, I wouldn't know what they were
saying. I don't speak Spanish, the second language of my sister's childhood. They appear to hold hands for a brief second
and my sister returns, grinning.

"We're next," she says.

"No, no, there's them and them," I say, hot and irritated
as I point to the stepfamily and the diabetic man and his wife.

"Trust me, we're next," Kathy says, adjusting her sun hat
a little to further shade her face. She is eight years older than
I, but her skin—fed since the mid-1980s on a steady diet of
the most expensive skin products—is creamy and smooth.

Just then the waiter lets out a whistle, and a van careens
to the curb. He speaks for a second to the driver, and then
the waiter and driver usher us into the first bench of seats.
The Midwestern man with his cane and his wife come
through the door next, hunched over with their floppy-
brimmed hats, inching past our able bodies to the only remaining seats on the back bench. On the sidewalk, the
waiter says something in Spanish to the stepfather. But the
man just gives him a blank stare until the waiter finally says
slowly in English, "You the next, Señor."

As we head up the road, I see the thirteen-year-old boy,
his tiny yellow headphones slung around his pink neck,
mouthing the words *I told you so* to his defeated stepfather.
I'm full of guilt and that complicated cocktail of injustice and
entitlement that is the drink of American tourists all over
the Third World. Still, I'm glad to be in the cool cab. It often

seems that to be an American here means to be at once greatly pleased and deeply ashamed. My sister is looking through her purse, nonplussed, in search of more pesos, no doubt. For her, this is not complicated.

A discussion between my sister, the driver, and the Midwestern couple behind us goes on for a few exchanges until it's clear to all of us that their resort is the first logical stop and ours will be the second. I relax for a minute, the guilt and heat subsiding, and take in the view of red, dusty soil and saguaros.

My sister's Spanish breaks the silence. I'm guessing the couple behind me is also staring sweaty and exhausted out the window and also has no idea what she's saying to the driver. I'm fine resting here in my heat-induced passivity, but then I hear a few words from my sister that I recognize: *hermana* (that's me), *enfermo* (I'm sick?), something something *pesos*. I look at my sister suspiciously. She doesn't return my gaze, just leans back in her seat and polishes her sunglasses with the tail of her blouse. A few minutes later the van hurtles into the driveway of *our* resort. I can't even look back at the Midwestern couple; as I slink out of the van, I keep my eyes trained on the back of Kathy's neatly pressed blouse.

This is her way. She learned this growing up here. I tend to think of it as her Mexican side, the part of her that knows how to work a system built on favor and exchange. But perhaps her ways are not so much the product of this particular culture as they are the traits of those raised in the school of survival everywhere. In every situation in which I'm uncertain, neurotic, apologizing to those who've done me wrong, she's quietly hustling all the angles, making sure she gets everything she needs and sometimes everything she wants as well. When our father visited her at the convent, she would say, "Please, Father, leave some extra money with the sisters for shampoo." That's what she has always called him: Father.

That was in the mid-sixties, a long time ago now. It was five years after my mother told my father she loved another man and he slapped her so hard one of her pearl earrings popped off and skittered like a pea across the hardwood floor of their California bungalow. She says she can't remember exactly how my father got custody of Kathy, but she can still, some forty years later, hear the echo of that pearl rolling across the floor.

I want to navigate this country with sentences of Spanish fully formed and falling off my tongue, like Kathy, but even as her sister, I have no claim to this language. She pulled these words into herself alone, as a child separated from her family and her country. When my parents divorced in 1962, I was less than a year old and she was eight. I had no words for what was happening, and she had only the stories an eight-year-old can tell herself, a fiction with a shape circumscribed by the stories of the day, by a short lifetime of books about Dick and Jane and Sally and *Look, Jane. Here comes Father now!* We can only tell ourselves about the parts of our lives for which we actually have words. As water must always take the shape of its container, the stories we tell can only take the form of the stories we already know.

Before she was ten, Kathy was fluent in Spanish. She can make even the serious waiters laugh in that genuine and confiding way they do with one another as they scrape our plates in the back of the restaurant. Every perfectly pronounced word she speaks says that we are not like the other tourists; we've earned this spot. In the States, I rarely hear her speak Spanish, and sometimes I half doubt that other words for *boyfriend, constellation,* and *mother* are really tucked inside her. I've only half-believed the rumors and whispered phrases about her childhood: *kidnapped . . . Mother Superior . . . in the convent.*

But here we are in Mexico, the country of her childhood, and every conversation reminds me that it's true. She really did grow up here in one convent and then another on the other side of this blue, blue Sea of Cortez that pulls the hot white sand out from under my feet. She's not just Kathleen; she's *Catalina,* too.

It's taken me about forty years to patch together this rudimentary chronology: In 1962, JoJo's father, James Chapman, died, and my father received a sizable hunk of stock—mostly shares of AT&T—worth about $100,000, a small fortune at the time. He used part of the money to purchase a ranch with horses and cattle a few hours northwest of Guadalajara, past the valleys of tequila's silver-blue agave plant, near a small village called Amatlán de Cañas. He hired a ranch hand named Pedro and moved to this place where no one spoke English in 1963 with his new wife, Lucille, and his share of the bounty from my parents' marriage—my sister, Kathy.

At this point the story loses coherence. I know my sister lived in two different convents between the ages of nine and fifteen, but when I try to understand how and why this happened, I feel like one of the blind men trying to describe the proverbial elephant—the big picture eludes me. My mother has her story. My sister has hers. My father's, for the most part, died with him in 1986. I do know that the little school in Amatlán didn't teach much, and that was my father's rationale for enrolling Kathy in the convent school fifty kilometers away, in Etzatlán. I know that Kathy lived in that remote corner of Jalisco for the next few years, attending convent schools, waiting for Father to sail into town with pesos, stamps, and soap, and forgetting all about Spot and Dick and little sister Sally.

BACK HOME IN SEATTLE, I FALL QUICKLY INTO THE routines of lethargy. Today Natalie, Jessie, and I are watching a movie, stretched out on the enormous marital bed. TV watching has become our number one pastime during this first winter of my divorce. The rain sweeps relentlessly against the windows of our old house, and I burrow a little deeper under the comforter beside my daughters and pretend the world is a warm and safe place as the soundtrack from *The Lizzie McGuire Movie* insists over and over that "this is what dreams are made of."

Natalie and Jess are nestled into each other, so accustomed to each other's presence that they don't seem to notice if one's arm crosses over the other's knee or if a head drops gradually down to rest on a sister's hip. It's not all sweetness like this. Not long ago, Jess squirmed naked under the bed to look for her hidden birthday present from Natalie. Natalie came in the room and spotted Jessie, and in one swift motion she went from pulling Jess's soft ankles to spanking her white bottom. I can see in these tussles how they take each other for granted, but their belief in the solidity of each other is also here now in all their sleepy gestures of elbows akimbo and head-nuzzled-into-armpit lounging. To me, every cell of their bodies seems to be saying this one thing: *She's there*.

Natalie is just about the same age Kathy was when my parents divorced. Kathy was nine when my father took her to Mexico; Natalie turned nine four days before her father and I split up. I want the similarities to end there. I don't want this divorce to leave my children with the legacy of unanswered questions that my parents' divorce bestowed upon me.

When my parents, Diane and Jack, met in 1952, they were both twenty-four and had one child apiece, the remnants of first marriages that ended nearly before they started. My mom's first marriage ended when she was twenty and in the first trimester of her first pregnancy. As a single mother, she couldn't support herself and her daughter, Susan, in Canada, so they left for the promised land of California, where they lived as boarders in another family's home. The landlady took care of Susan during the day while Diane worked as a teller at a bank. She had two work dresses. She wore one one day and the other the next. Maybe one was powdery blue with a stripe of navy and the other kelly green, the green a child might color a Christmas tree. Back then women could wear colors like that, bright and brilliant, without irony or embarrassment. Earrings and purse to match, even.

Maybe it was the blue one she wore the day Jack came into the bank. She was counting bills (twenty-one, twenty-two, twenty-three), when she sensed someone in front of her teller's cage. "They match," he said when she looked up, "the dress and your eyes." He had black hair, tan skin, and eyes that were dark brown with little flecks of green. He was a smooth operator, a salesman with a convertible out front. It would take only a few days before she would meet him in front of the bank at closing time, get into his car, and speed away into the future and her second marriage.

They had a reputation as a fun couple, a couple with a boat and a penchant for parties. Their construction company was growing. On the weekends their little house filled for cocktail parties and barbecues. Grown-ups crowded into the living room with their manhattans and martinis; children streaked through sprinklers and drank root beer floats in the backyard. My mother was the envy of the other mothers on the block because she was beautiful and had enough money for a nanny, but there was a wildness about her that threatened to shake their ordered lives. She laughed a little too hard; she flirted with the other husbands and poured a stronger drink than the other women. "And that oldest girl," neighbors whispered, "you know she has a different father." My mother was a divorcée in a time when people still used that word.

Photos of my parents show a glamorous couple, a man with black hair combed neatly and his blond wife with eyes the color of a Canadian sky. Here they are twined together on a motorcycle, waving and grinning in the convertible, now on the boat, my mother playing skipper at the wheel with the captain's hat tilted at a sexy angle. Here they are all dressed up for the country club talent show the night they sang, "Frankie and Johnny were lovers / Oh Lordy how they could love."

It's hard to reconcile these happy pictures with the facts of their marriage. They were two stubborn only children, neither suited for the sacrifices marriage inevitably requires. They were unfaithful, he with many women and she with one man. In their nine years of marriage they had three more children, all daughters, all unplanned in that *I Love Lucy* way (Lucy: Ricky, I'm pregnant! Ricky: Bab-a-loo!), in the days long before commercials for the birth-control patch, before the word *ovulation* was batted about in public places.

Their first daughter, Kathy, was born in the honeymoon days—1953. In 1955 they had another daughter, Jackie, who died at just eight months, following surgery to remove a defective kidney. I grew up with a little white teddy bear of hers. If I wound it up, it played the song of my mother's sadness, "Brahms' Lullaby." A few years after Jackie died, just months before their divorce, one more daughter was born.

They had their grief. They had their anger and they both had their guilt. They had a red convertible, a boat, a business, lovers and lawyers, and then, just before it all exploded, before all the atoms blew out to their separate places in the universe, they had me.

A few months before he died, my father told me his version of what happened in 1962. We were sitting in his backyard in the blue Northern California light. It was several years into his fourth marriage, two years after he'd joined AA, and a few weeks after cancer began to course through his body. Against the house's white stucco wall, dusty, overripe tomatoes drooped from their vines, threatening to tumble to the ground and split in two. He said that when they divorced, my mother took my thirteen-year-old half sister, Susan, Kathy, and me, but then one day he asked himself, Why am I giving up Kathy? So he went back to my mother's flat-roofed California apartment and took Kathy, just as his grandfather, James Chapman, had gone back to his ex-wife's house to take his daughter, JoJo, to live with him.

There was a silence, and then I went for the safe and the obvious: I asked him about his childhood in Redwood City in the thirties. But he didn't answer. He just looked right at me and answered the question I could not ask: "You were just a baby, so of course I couldn't take you."

I've often imagined what this scene between my parents must have looked like the day my dad came for Kathy. It is late 1962. Silicon Valley before the silicon, when walnut orchards peppered the landscape and lemon trees lined the streets. Probably it is a sunny afternoon, the clouds just wispy ribbons in the sky above. He puts the top down, turns up a Johnny Mathis song on the radio, and drives down the Bayshore toward Mountain View, the turn signal blinking her name—*Kath-y, Kath-y, Kath-y*.

Susan's in a back room, sipping Dr Pepper and laughing into the phone, and Kathy's in the kitchen, flipping through a Richie Rich comic book. In my imagination, we are to-gether nonstop in those post-divorce days, sealed into an unrelenting, apartment-size version of family life, a mother and three daughters huddled together. On every horizon, girlfamily is all we see.

Embedded in this scene is the childish romantic notion that we are important and we are hiding from something— like the Franks in their secret attic. There's a knock at the door, and my mother answers it with the baby—me— swaddled in the crook of her arm. My father angles in, lead-ing with one shoulder like Jack Lord on *Hawaii Five-O*. He looks right past me, refusing to be lured in by my sirenlike baby beauty.

Kathy closes her comic, stands, and tugs the back of her bathing suit bottom a little. "Daddy," she says.

But then what? Does he say simply, "Get in the car, Kathy. I need to speak with your mother"? Or does he say, as fathers in old movies might if those movies were about fathers claiming their daughters from their mothers, "Get your stuff, kid. You're coming with me"?

And what about my mother? Does she wail, weep, hold

on to my sister's scrawny eight-year-old self, and shout, like a desperate Sally Field, "Like hell you're taking her!" Or does she say, sullenly, like a girl who's lost a protracted game of Monopoly, "Okay, then," and pull out an old suitcase? Maybe she drops in underpants, a sundress the color of dandelions, a black-and-white snapshot of herself. Kathy's excited like she's going to Disneyland. Her sandals slap, slap, slap as she runs down the hall to tell Susan. I'm lucky. I'm a baby, too young to be sad, to notice the hole my father and sister are blasting through my life.

My father and Kathy moved back to the States when I was eight, to a town near ours in the Bay Area. I wanted badly for my sister to come live with us, but she never did. My mother said there were some things a child couldn't understand, and this was one of them. She never did come to live with us, and I soon learned that the distance between Mountain View and Menlo Park was almost as great as the divide between Mountain View and Etzatlán. She belonged to my father and I belonged to my mother. Our lives would be separate no matter what the geographical distance, our orbits crossing only when the sun and the moon aligned just so.

5

Down the Rabbit Hole

Today is the last day I will see Kevin before we are legally separated. If all goes well today in this courtroom of blond oak and green carpeting, I will sail out of here with my legal separation safely recorded in the annals of King County. My attorney says he's never seen someone in such a hurry to get this done. He has this infuriating way of saying things like, "*Someone's* in a rush!" But today I don't care. The fire burning under my feet is that I'm not positive—even after seeing the credit report—that I know the full extent of Kevin's debts, and the separation agreement stipulates that all the credit card debt he accrued without my knowledge will be his sole financial responsibility. Over the last manic eleven days, I've thought of this race to get this paper signed, sealed, and delivered as Operation Save the House. The attorney says that even with the agreement, creditors could still come after me if Kevin doesn't make good on his debts, but that I'll be in a lot better position than I would be without it. Someone's in a rush, indeed.

Despite the warm day, I'm bundled in my black wool coat. As I come through the glass doors of the courthouse, I catch sight of a reflection of myself—black coat, scarf draped around my neck, dark sunglasses, expression some-what stricken—and see a woman I don't know, a woman in a black-and-white movie, wronged but perhaps not fatally so, certain that a reversal of fortune can be expected be-fore the credits roll. But once inside, all hope for the future drains from me as I take in the scene of dreary but excru-ciating real life—security guards yawning, mothers with babies on their blanketed shoulders, lawyers squeezing re-luctantly into elevators with plaintiffs and defendants, look-ing vaguely annoyed to find themselves shoulder-to-shoulder with the rabble.

I see my lawyer and sit beside him on one of the back benches of the courtroom. We whisper for a few minutes about what will happen next. He can barely remember my name or the details of my case. When we were working through a plan for division of property last week, he said, "You wouldn't believe how many women come through here and are utterly shocked to hear they're going to have to give up the country club." I looked at him flatly and thought, If I hadn't just paid twenty-one dollars to park in this fucking building, I would walk out of here right now. And then I said, "Oh, interesting," and we got back to work.

Kevin comes in and sidles in beside me, like we're at a

play, or at the funeral of a distant acquaintance. Now blister-
ingly hot but too cramped to unbutton my coat, I'm sandwiched in between two men who—at least for this
moment—I despise. I'm a blazing tower of malevolence
held together by a black wool coat.

The judge calls our names, and the three of us trudge to
the front. The judge asks me if I'm seeking a legal separation
from my husband and I say I am. The formation is the same
as it was on our wedding day; I'm on the judge's right and
Kevin's on his left. The minister who stood in this space between us some eleven and a half years ago said ours would
be a marriage of joy and laughter. And for a long time it was.

The judge shuffles and stamps and shuffles and stamps
until at last he's done. He hands our papers to my lawyer and
we all walk away. I bolt out of the courtroom so I won't have
to ride down in the same elevator as Kevin. I don't say good-
bye or anything. I just leave. I tell myself it's because my class
starts in an hour at the university. But I'm sure I'm rushing
because I don't want whatever I'm going to feel next to
catch up to me. If I move very quickly, maybe I can fast-
forward straight to the end of this B-movie, right into the
arms of my reversal of fortune.

THIS MOVIE NEVER DOES CUT TO THE CHASE, THOUGH. It
creeps forward frame by frame, a child's flip-book released
in surreal slow motion. A few still images of me heaving
laundry from washer to dryer, maybe another of driving the

kids to school, flipping through the stations in search of the song that won't evoke rage or despair, the occasional glamorous shot of me staring, slack-jawed, into the vacant middle distance. Sometimes, unbidden, the movie rewinds and starts up once again from the very first shots of boy meets girl. Even when it seems like I've lost interest in the whole dreary business, the mind remains pretty much indefatigable in its search for answers to the questions *why* and *how*.

The first time Kevin came to my house it was a Saturday morning. Six months earlier I'd traded my life in San Francisco as a waitress and grad student for professordom in a small town in Utah. Saturdays were something of a relief from teaching and from the snug insularity of the town, but they could also be long. I'd made friends with a couple of women who worked at the college, but they were busy on the weekends with husbands and children, so on weekend days I organized drawers, exercised, and wrote in my journal like a fourteen-year-old girl away for the summer. On this Saturday morning I was walking down the hall of my little house when I spotted a glint of something, a bare patch between the green carpeting and the wall, that caught my eye.

I pulled up a little corner of this bright green shabby carpet and saw it: the mother lode. Hardwood so beautiful, so shiny and golden, it made me weak. Maybe I could have a bit of my old San Francisco life right here in the heart of paneling-and-linoleum country, in this landlocked place where innocent wood floors like these could be suffocated under a heavy layer of shag. Maybe, I thought, my house could be my sanctuary from the brutalities of the super-conservative, small-town reality just outside my door.

Much as I loved the new job, giving up cultural diversity, great movie houses, the Tassajara Bakery, Golden Gate Park, and the cafés of North Beach often seemed like too great a price to pay. But it wasn't just the trappings of San Francisco I missed. I longed for people from my own tribe—people who knew gay was as good as straight, preferred bookstores to rodeos, and could describe the word *alienation* using personal examples. As Bill Maher has said, "There's a lot of blue people in red states," and suddenly I was one of them.

Without a real plan, I began yanking the carpet back with passion. Out, out, I would get the green beast out of there. There was a touch of madness in this yanking, a malaise a tad worse than a bad case of cabin fever. I tore and I tore. The bottom of the carpeting was covered in something that looked like rubber cement. Little carpeting nails held the carpeting down at the perimeter of the room, and some of them were determined to stay lodged into the floor, but if I pulled hard enough and wedged a kitchen knife under the stubborn ones, they popped out and the carpet yielded a little more. As I yanked, I pushed the carpet into a large, gummy roll.

The ugly green roll quickly gained in size until I could only heave the thing away from me inch by slow inch. Soon it took over the room at a diagonal, like a giant cigar dividing the room. I realized then, yes, *way* too late, that I'd never be able to get the wretched beast out of the house even if I did get it completely torn away from the floor. I estimated the carpet's total weight to be about 650 pounds. I was exhausted, hungry, and a little depressed. I lay on the giant thing for a minute, sweating, feeling stuck in so many ways. How had this become my life? Why was there always something heavy and impossible between me and what I wanted? Then there was a knock on the door.

There had been a few knocks on the door when I first moved to town. The only single women my age were divorced and had a few handfuls of children. Without crediting myself too much, I can safely say that someone like me had never moved to this town before, partly because someone like me, in her right mind, would not and should not choose such a place for her home. At the college where I taught, I was constantly asked if I was the secretary to the male professor with whom I shared an office. Townsfolk frequently asked me disturbing questions, their faces twisted in confusion over the course of my life, "So after college you did *what?*" "And you've *never* been married?" Anywhere else I was pretty ordinary—a single twenty-nine-year-old woman fresh from grad school—but in this town I was an exotic bird, my bright feathers sticking out everywhere I went.

In the first few weeks I met all of the town's eligible bachelors vaguely in my age range. There were three: one an alcoholic, one with an obvious penchant for seventeen-year-olds, and another a religious zealot. Each found a reason to knock on the door, and each was sent off in the direction whence he came. But that was months earlier.

I pulled back the curtain. It was Kevin, whom I'd flirted with recklessly at the college last week. He was a student who'd come from California at the beginning of the school year. He didn't fit into the local scene any more than I did. He was twenty-two, a hair older than most of the other students, but still way too young for me. At least he wasn't in any of my classes.

"Hi. I was walking by and I saw your car. I thought I'd say hi." He seemed a little nervous. He'd taken a big chance, knocking on my door, and I didn't believe for a minute that he was "just walking by," even though I did live in the middle of town.

I looked over at the driveway. My car was old and very ugly, a 1980 Monte Carlo that was one shade darker than primer. No one in town had a vehicle like this. The convenience-store clerks had better cars than mine. This was a town where half your monthly income was supposed to go toward a car payment for something new, red, and shiny.

"Well, hey," I stammered. "Uh, you wanna come in?"

He came into the front room, his eyes moving back and forth between clammy me and the cigar of carpeting. "What are you doing?" He asked it slowly, as if I were a child caught doing something she shouldn't.

I sunk into the couch. "I want these hardwoods, see. They have something of San Francisco in them. I want this carpet gone."

"Okay, okay," he said. He started walking around the place as he spoke, calling to me from the kitchen, the hall, the bedroom. He had the measured walk of a contractor making a bid. He had many questions, hard questions, questions I should've thought of on my own: Was I sure the wood was good in all the rooms? Would the property manager mind that I was pulling up the carpeting? Was there a place, a dry place, the carpet could be stored? A basement, maybe?

"I don't know," I said in a quiet voice.

"What do you mean you don't know?" He was the student. He saw me as the professor. He was showing a little bravado by turning things around and asking me the questions, but I'm sure he expected that I would know what I was doing.

"I don't know the answers to any of those questions." I noticed then that he had the endearing good looks of a handsome man who's completely unaware of how he appears to others.

"O-kay," he said, letting a breath out. Then he smiled brightly and asked, "So, do you want help?"

"You think you can? But hey, I don't want to take your time. I'm sure you need to study or something." I was a little embarrassed on the word *study*, the word that pointed to the difference between us, to the fact that he should be off with the young at the tennis court or the library and I should be sealed off in my self-sufficient professorial life.

"I want to." He smiled again, slowly this time. He seemed so familiar, like someone I recognized but couldn't place. I didn't want him to leave, but I was also afraid of what might happen if he stayed. By the time I'd managed to say *all right,* he was at work on the horrible task of expelling the big, bad green carpet from my house.

Work, pure backbreaking work, is an underestimated element of the magic of attraction. During that long day of furniture moved out and in, of carpet cutting, rolling, and dragging, of floor washing and waxing, it dawned on me how little had been done on my behalf until then. No man had so much as helped me move. All of a sudden the boy-friends of my twenties seemed terribly anemic and selfish: a wannabe rock-and-roll boy who had eaten my groceries and smoked my cigarettes, a writer who'd been too plagued by stress, fatigue, and carpal tunnel to do anything much for me. I'd lived for a long time in that cool world of too proud to ask and too lazy to offer.

I was won over by work, not just that day but in those that followed. If I idly mentioned a household project, Kevin would say, "Okay, let's get started," and a few minutes later we'd be headed out the door and over to the Ben Franklin store for paint or nails, like a newlywed couple. It was more than his capability that pulled me in; it was the sheer get-up-and-go. When faced with a large task, I was a person prone to rocking in the middle of the floor and chanting, "It can't be done." No one had ever disagreed with me on this point before, but now here was this human tornado of energy and, well, youth, come to pull me out of my dark hole. He was so generous by nature, so innocent of the world I was from, the domain of the cool guy, that I felt a little guilty, like I should say to him, "Did you know that there are grown men who get away with doing half what you do, who would just as soon watch MTV for an afternoon as do something for someone else?"

It was spring when we went from friends to more. We were watching a movie on the sofa and we kept sitting closer and closer and closer until finally we kissed. Once the threshold was crossed, we knew that was it. There would be no dating other people; we were going to be together. Summer came early in that little town that year, and with all the warm sunshine and birds cheeping, we were swallowed whole by this blue-skied happiness where Bob Marley was perpetually singing about the benefits of relaxation and redemption. We kept all the windows and doors open while we painted my kitchen the pink and yellow of Easter eggs. We planted red geraniums in front of the house and then wandered down the street to pick up groceries for dinner.

We tore ourselves away from our little paradise to go to work and school, and then rushed back to my house at day's end. The outside world was problematic. I didn't exactly think I could hide our relationship, but I wasn't ready to announce that the new English instructor who was already considered suspect had taken on a student lover seven years her junior.

One night during dinner, Paula came to the door. Paula was another suspicious character in town. She was the other young and female instructor at the college, and although she was married, she too was under constant scrutiny. Her primary crime was that she taught math, a subject a pretty girl shouldn't be good at, and she wasn't just pretty in a regular way but in an over-the-top, lingerie-model kind of way.

I opened the door a crack. "Hey, Paula."

"So are you ready?"

I noticed then that she was in workout clothes. "Oh God, the gym, that's right. I forgot. Maybe tomorrow?"

I still had the door open just enough for my head to peek through. She gestured with her head toward the inside and lowered her brows a little. "Who's in there? Houseboy? Houseboy's the reason you can't go to the gym, isn't he?"

"Paula, *shhhh!* What are you thinking? C'mon. We'll go to the gym tomorrow. I'm sorry. I am."

She accepted this, finally, and started down my front steps, but she was still making some noises, audible inside no doubt, noises akin to a third grader's rendition of "Someone's Got a Boyfriend."

I closed the door quickly, bolted it, and returned to the table, saying something absurd like, "Now, where were we?"

"I heard what she said. *Houseboy?* Is that what you think?" He wasn't mad exactly. He asked in this calm, even way, which somehow made me feel worse.

"No! That's just Paula, you know, she's kind of crazy." She wasn't kind of crazy. She was, in fact, a sort of rational, reason-driven person. We both knew this. It was me who was kind of crazy. I was the one who didn't want to think things through. I was the one who was allowing our lives to become entwined without thinking of the consequences.

"So do you picture yourself with me in five years?" He was smiling at me now, a nervous smile.

"In five years! That's a job interview question. You know," I made my voice deep, "and tell us, Ms., Ms., what is it, ah yes, Ms. Hanratty, where do you imagine yourself in five years?" I was frantic, feeling exposed by Paula's *houseboy* comment. I was just about to launch into another voice, the high-pitched one of the interviewee explaining her vision for five years hence, when he grabbed both my hands.

"I'm serious. I, I adore you."

I adore you. I'd never heard words like this before. *I adore you.* Was it English? It sounded like French, or perhaps an antique version of English. How had he thought of something so beautiful to say? It was simpler, clearer, purer than the words *I love you,* which were used by nearly everyone and seemed to require the words *I love you too* in return.

The words came to me slowly like I was underwater and calling through a tunnel to the surface above, but finally I got them out. "I want to be together," I said, at last.

ONE DAY WE WERE ON A WALK THROUGH THE HOT SUMMER streets of the town and ended up on the shaded swings at the playground. Giant maples ringed this Norman Rockwell–style park with its little white gazebo in the middle. Kevin watched the children who ran from slide to swing to jungle gym with a happy and surprised look on his face, as though he'd never seen such a scene before. From the other side of the park, anyone could see at a glance that Kevin was a person who wanted children. He would be a father one day, with or without me. But I stayed as far away as I could from that subject.

It was a Sunday—the day when we often had long picnics while the rest of the town was in church. We ate bagels and napped on a big blanket. He'd bring his homework and I'd bring my grading. We worked side by side, maybe just a couple of feet twined together. We told each other stories from our childhoods. His family had its share of divorce, loss, and sadness, but mostly they'd been happy. He came from a world of Boy Scouts and soap-box derbies, a sunny Southern California suburb crowded with children running in and out of one another's houses. His family went on camping vacations, towing the family tent trailer behind them as they wound their way through the tawny California hills—Dad at the helm, Mom riding shotgun, kids packed side by side in the back.

That day we talked about the heat, the end of the school year, our plan to visit his mother in San Diego that summer, until the conversation turned to someone we knew, a student from Mexico City who'd recently become a father. His girlfriend in Mexico had had a baby boy a few weeks before, and he'd just come back from a trip to see them.

"He's a lucky man," Kevin called to me, as he pumped his swing up a little higher in the air.

"Lucky man! Good Lord, you're kidding. He's still an undergrad. He wants to be an architect, so now he's going to be supporting these two through four more years of school. At least. What, on student loans?" The naïveté of Kevin's comment annoyed me. It was evidence for those who believed he was too young for me. I hoped those people were wrong. I wanted him to be right about the benevolence of the universe, but I needed him to prove it to me, so I added for good measure, "He doesn't even know if he wants to marry her!" as my swing fell backward past his.

"The details will work out or they won't."

"Oh, there you go! I'm sure that'll be a great comfort for the child," I called. I wanted to see if there was any substance to his optimism, some reasoning that I could bank on, arguments I could maybe even use to combat my own pessimism about life and my fear of family.

"He'll get a job at night, probably."

"So go to school all day, work all night? That's a tough plan."

"I don't know how they'll do it," he said. "It probably won't be easy."

"I'll say."

"It will be hard, but he'll have that child and his love for him forever, no matter what. The details don't matter. It'll work out."

Such young idealism! The details don't matter! Let's see how much the details don't matter when you're working at a job you hate to pay the mortgage, I wanted to say. But I was silent. I kept swinging, higher now, my feet pointed to the sky, nearly reaching that mythic place at the top of the swing's arc. When I was a child, kids said if you went over the top, you'd end up in another land, another life. You wouldn't even remember who you were.

"It isn't supposed to be easy," he said. I thought then about Kevin's father, how he'd died suddenly, mysteriously, just days before Kevin's tenth birthday. Kevin's family had planned to celebrate after his dad got out of the hospital, but he hadn't come home. Kevin never had his birthday that year. He was young, but he did know something about hard, about having less than you need.

His swing had slowed to a stop. He was standing now, his feet on the ground, his arms twisted in the swing's chains.

"But the best things are hard," he said, watching me go back and forth. "The things that make you happy, you have to work for them."

How simple was that? *The things that make you happy you have to work for.* There were probably ordinary people milling about, walking in and out of offices and grocery stores, who knew this, who'd known this for a long time even, who lived like it was true. And here before me was this twenty-two-year-old who knew this and already lived like it was true.

I'm from a long line of stock-market speculators, artists of unmarketable talent, and alcoholics. The higher, harder road is not our road. We move, we divorce, we drink, or we disappear. And our children, some of them, have slipped from our custody. We tell a good story. We swing between the poles of festive and melancholy. We are not a people who have worked for happiness.

That night I couldn't sleep. I was counting the flaws of this man-child who slept so soundly beside me. First of all, I decided, he was absurdly young. He hadn't lived enough, hadn't even finished college. He took laundry out of the dryer before it was all the way dry. He was too young. He probably didn't even know who Jean-Paul Sartre and Simone de Beauvoir were. He didn't know that *vino* meant wine. How in the hell could a person not know that? Who *didn't* know that? How did you even get to be twenty-two years old and never come across the word *vino*? And he talked to his mom too much on the phone. I mean, what's to talk about? I did this, Mom, how's that, Mom? A grown person shouldn't talk to his mom that much. And another thing: When he put the dishes away, he put the mugs with bowls and the bowls with mugs. Come on! Mugs with mugs!

And besides, he was too young.

I leaned over him. "Are you awake?"

No answer. How could I possibly link my fate to someone who could slumber through the Apocalypse? He would never catch that first scent of fire if I relaxed and missed it. It was one more for the list: sleeping habits of teenage boy! Impossible to wake up in the morning. Although, admittedly, this was not truly morning—1:40 a.m., actually.

"Are you awake?" I said again, louder this time.

"No," he said flatly and rolled over.

"Could you be? Could you wake up? I'm upset."

"Okay," he said, groggily, half propping himself up on pillows. "What is it?"

He looked so sweet. Lord, forgive me for my sins, I thought. Forgive me for the anguish I'm about to inflict on another human being.

"What's wrong?"

"I don't know," I said.

"Well, what do you think it is?"

"This isn't going to work," I said. "I'm not like you. Everything is simple in your world. Things are complicated for me, it's my own fault, but I can't help it and I don't think I can stop."

I believed this and I didn't. I was in a dark space, but I was also the sniper who wanted someone to talk her down.

"Too big. Too black," he said and started to close his eyes again.

I scooted over to him. "Aren't you going to say anything about this? Aren't you concerned?"

"I don't know where to start. Tell me one thing you can say for sure is wrong."

"You talk to your mom too much on the phone," I blurted out.

He looked at me like I was Lucifer, and I could feel little horns sprouting through my scalp. "I love my mom. And besides she's older and lives alone," he said.

"Good answer. Okay, this is what I mean. For you, things are really, really simple. You love your mom and so you call her. And for me things are very muddy, like I love my mom and so I don't always call her and when I do call her I get frustrated with her and she gets frustrated with me and so then I don't call her and then I feel guilty and then I call her."

"So you're saying you'd rather be with someone like you," he said, and then added in a patronizing tone, "someone complicated."

"When you put it that way, it sounds very bad. See, that's the thing. I don't want to go through the rest of my life feeling like I'm the difficult one, the one who makes things complicated."

"If you were with someone difficult, you could be the easy one," he offered.

"Yes, but I would get tired of them being difficult and I would leave."

He was silent for an extra beat. "And you think I will get tired of you and leave you, but I won't ever leave you. I won't ever hurt you."

I looked at Kevin, at the outline of his face in my dark bedroom, and said, "You say that but you don't *know*, do you?"

"You can fight it if you want, but it's not complicated."

"It's not?"

"No, it's not," he said, sliding all the way back down into the pillows.

Then all at once I felt very tired and ready to go back to sleep. But I lay there for a few minutes after he'd drifted off again. I wanted to take in his belief in simplicity, in the way things should be, and make it my own.

A year later we were married. The forces that would

keep us together for twelve years and those that would tear us apart were already in place, invisible to us but quietly and constantly at work. It was his energy and positivity that got us through all the long days and nights of our daughters' baby and toddler years, but it was also his energy that took him to card houses late at night, that powered him through endless poker games. Kevin's sunny optimism gave me faith enough to put my skepticism and fear aside and make the leap into family life. But it was also his insistence that the details would work out that allowed him to get into the habit of gambling money he didn't have. I guess he kept thinking that he would be able to make everything okay no matter what.

But he couldn't and neither could I.

6

Welcome to Divorce 101

The Girl Scout leader who's conducting the annual Cookie Kickoff meeting tonight wears a corduroy pinafore dress alarmingly close in color to the deep forest green of the Junior's uniform. Her hair, clipped short in a utilitarian bob, is the graying middle brown that would no doubt be my own hair color if I didn't spend big money to have it dyed and highlighted every seven weeks. It's been only a few months since Kevin and I separated, and I'm fixated on the abundance of wedding rings all around me. As my grandmother JoJo used to say, "To the pickpocket, all the world is pockets." This woman's wedding ring—a plain gold band, of course—shows no trace of girlish indulgence or whimsy. I recognize her at a glance as one of those I've often referred to as "the rules people."

The rules people are the men and women who have enough self-control to follow instructions, safety guidelines, and, more generally, the principles that ensure success in endeavors that involve accuracy and discipline. The rules people completed their general-ed requirements during their first two years of college before gorging themselves on all the enticing courses in their majors; they did not, like me, have to take a course crowded with football players called "Math Games" in their fifth year of college because it was the only way to fulfill the math requirement and graduate. When the rules people join Weight Watchers, they actually lose weight because they understand—as one understands that plants need water and light to grow—that they cannot eat above their daily "point" allotment and still lose weight. The rules people generally do not spend twelve dollars a week to attend the Weight Watchers meeting and then day after day eat a few points over the limit "just to see" if the system will still work. The rules people are capable of losing more than five pounds after twelve weeks of Weight Watchers. It does not cost them $144 to end up with their jeans just a fraction looser.

For a long time I've been aware of the crucial differences between the rule followers and lackadaisical people like me. And tonight—squirming here in my chair through a long lecture on this year's new cookie, boothing guidelines, and the inviolable ten-day window known as "presales"—I wonder: Does it really happen to them? They say it can happen to anyone, but is that actually true? Surely these incredibly sensible women, the women who would never dream of buying a laptop on impulse, who really do shop around for the lowest price on car insurance, who majored in biology or earth sciences, who measure dry ingredients when baking and actually own the metal spatula utensil used to level off the heaping cup of flour, are immune to some of this divorce misery.

If they're not immune, I can't believe that their odds aren't quite favorable of picking a mate with a similar passion for recycling, CPR training, and driving within the speed limit. These women think things through. They do not spend money all December and then bicker all the way through January. They have a Christmas savings account.

My mind has been locked up in just this sort of twisted thinking these past few weeks. Well, more specifically, I've been engaging in a struggle between this incessant habit of comparing myself to others and the knowledge that to do so is insanely irrational and that struggle and suffering are part of the universal experience, even if the struggle of others isn't always evident to me. Similarly, my brain has hosted a war between a faction that insists that marriage is a doomed institution to which no one is truly suited and a hostile tribe that is adamant that the true problem resides in my innate inability to grasp the laws of cause and effect—that if only I'd majored in accounting, if only I were one of the rules people, I wouldn't be divorced and unemployed at this age.

This habit of comparing myself with others has dogged me all my life. As a kid, I was obsessed with the ease with which certain kids seemed to sail through their days. Why was I forever falling off my bike and losing my homework?

How were other kids staying on their bikes? What was keeping them there? I remember in the eleventh grade, I sat my friend Cathie Webster down and said, "How do you do it? How do you make everything look so easy?" She had long straight blond hair and the members of her family were named in descending alphabetical order from oldest daughter, Anita, to middle daughter, Barbie, and then the youngest, Cathie. Like most of the families in our über-Anglican neighborhood, their family tree had no severed limbs; no divorces had divided their loyalties or their attention. But as smart as Cathie was, she had no idea what I was talking about, even though I explained my entire neurosis ad nauseam.

"Okay," I said finally, "just tell me how it is you get straight As. Like in Mr. Callow's social studies class, how is it I am always getting C-pluses on the essays and you're always getting As?"

"That's easy," she said, "I just write exactly what he says in class, the same words and everything. I just feed it right back to him."

I sat there dumbfounded for a minute. "You mean like you can actually hear what he says?" Earlier that month we'd been assigned *All Quiet on the Western Front*. I'd actually read it, which I thought was commendable, but I had no idea what Mr. Callow had said about it. To me, he sounded like the teacher in the *Peanuts* specials: *waaaw, waaaw, waaaaw.*

"Well, of course, can't you?" she asked.

"No, I can't," I said, and I realized then that I hadn't heard any of my teachers in years. It was like I was swimming underwater during class, hearing nothing but the muffled roar of the voices above and the deafening sound of my own thoughts. I guess that was the difference between kids like Cathie and me; I was so busy wondering whether I was okay that I couldn't attend to the world around me, while Cathie— she just knew she was okay and that she was the C of *ABC*.

PARTLY IT'S BECAUSE DIVORCE IS RELATIVELY UNCOMMON in my little circle here in Seattle that I sometimes see myself self-pityingly as the lone divorcée among the snug little familial knots of three and four playing Frisbee in every park and heading up to the ski slopes in their Subarus. And partly my new status as "the divorced one" is an emotional flashback to how I grew up.

When my mother remarried in 1971, we moved from California to a conservative Canadian neighborhood where divorce was uncommon. I only knew of one other divorced kid in my neighborhood, and people talked about her family with the same hushed surprise that they probably used when they spoke of mine, if they ever did at all. Risqué topics like divorce were not spoken of in this Vancouver suburb of strong hot tea and sweaters hand-knitted by someone's aunt back in Wiggin or Edinburgh. An outbreak of eyebrow-raising and throat-clearing would usually extinguish any conversation that wandered onto the topic of someone's particularly human and public failing.

And now I admit that my thoughts stray once again to *look how easy it is for them* when I see the married moms pull up after school in vehicles still maintained by manufacturers' warranties. But, overall, this divorce business has become a lesson in the humanity of us all and in letting go of the adolescent part of me that still wants to believe that no struggle is as compelling or as difficult as my own.

One cold, stormy Sunday, the *New York Times* publishes an essay I've written titled "The Chicken's in the Oven, My Husband's Out the Door." The next morning I wake up to an e-mail box full of letters from readers. I'm scared to open the first one. I'm pretty sure it will say, "Quit your whining!" And the next will surely read, "Buck up—don't you know there are people out here with real problems?" But I get myself a cup of tea, steel myself for the worst sort of criticism, and click on the first one, which has the subject line "Second Chances." The e-mail begins, "Maybe you're still fumbling around in those rooms like sorrow and suchlike, but when you find the back door and escape you might be surprised at what can be waiting out there. I was forty-two, overweight, mother to two mostly grown children when I found myself single. It was one of the long falling-apart ones. It needed to happen."

The reader goes on to tell how she met her current husband and how they've been happily married for the last ten years. For some reason I'm enormously touched that she's included the detail that she had been overweight, as if she were saying, "See just how bad things were for me and still they turned around?" She ends the letter with the wisdom and affection of an older friend: "Good luck to you. It'll wear you out, but you'll survive."

I put down my cup of tea. I feel like I've been shaken out of myself. I imagine what it must have been like ten years ago for this mother of two, how she had once been heading into an unknown future as I am now. I'm touched that this woman—now safely ensconced in a happy marriage—has taken the time to write to a stranger on the road behind her.

I open another e-mail. It's from a reader who describes the uncanny similarities between her situation and my own, how strangely she, too, had been roasting a chicken at the moment of her marriage's final fissure. I begin to tear through the mountain of e-mails, and while a couple tell me to quit my sniveling, the bulk of them resound with supportive cheers of "Me too!" and "Keep on trucking, Sister!" I'm surprised that just as many men as women have written to me. Because of Kevin's anger with me, I've imagined that there is something about me now that is loathsome to men, something that has flung me out of the scope of any man's empathy, so their confidences of marriages gone bad and words of kindness feel particularly reassuring. One reader suggests I get a body pillow to sleep beside, so I won't feel quite so alone. Others offer career advice, dating suggestions, encouragement and prayers, and the details of their own stories—all filled with the same astonished grief that has been the constant refrain of my own divorce.

My heart goes out to all the readers who've written to me not only of their loss but also of the strange ambivalence divorce can bring. One man writes this about his ex-wife:

> *I've been divorced for 15 years. I had been married for 23. Driving home one night a week ago from dinner with my ex-wife, with whom I have an amiable, comfortable, arm's-length relationship, I suddenly realized from one little phrase in a song on the radio that I'm still a bit in love with her. It's a nice feeling because we were once very much in love but tears formed in my eyes because I knew in the same moment there was nothing to be done about it.*

I am haunted by the image of this man riding in the dark thinking wistfully about the woman to whom he was once married, by this small proof of the heart's tenacious memory. It's hard to conceive of the enormity of the toll of marriage gone awry. How many of us live not just with heartbreak and despair, but also with the grainier, grittier successors of loss—nagging ambivalence, alienation, isolation, and ennui?

I feel as though I've joined an enormous club, something like the Veterans of Foreign Wars. We are weary with battle fatigue and sometimes even gripped by nostalgia for the good old, bad old days, but our numbers are large. We've all heard over and over again that some 50 percent of all marriages end in divorce, but I find it astonishing to think of the sheer numbers of us who have been inducted into this club. About 10 percent of the American population is divorced. As of

2000, there were about twenty million divorced Americans, about as many as the entire population of the state of Texas at that time.

The dark flip side of the booming wedding industry, divorce has become a multibillion-dollar industry, with the legal work alone accounting for "a staggering 28 billion dollar[s] a year," according to an article that appeared on forbes.com in September 2005. A Google search using the word *divorce* brings up platoons of hits, with sites offering everything from sketchy legal advice ("Start your legal separation online today!") to a shot at meeting your next mate. I find singleparentsmingle.com and singleparents.com, with their images of cheery, corn-fed looking men and women hooking up with a child or two wedged between them, rather unnerving. It's a nice enough idea—starting over with this fresh-faced person who apparently loves children as much as you do and who seems to show no signs of the strain associated with child-support payments or a work schedule that competes with his parenting one—but here on earth the divorce rate for second marriages involving children hovers around 60 percent.

More than a million children are involved in new divorces in this country each year, and, according to the research done by the Centers for Disease Control (CDC), one of the key factors that determine the likelihood of divorce is the marital status of your family of origin. In a sample of study participants of women from all races, there was a

29 percent chance that a first marriage would break up within ten years for those participants from intact families of origin, and a 43 percent chance of divorce for those women from divorced families. Other sources give even more weight to the theory that divorce is something that gets passed down along with the family cabin in Idaho and Grandma's teacup collection. According to the statistics gathered by divorce-source.com, children of divorce are 50 percent more likely to end up divorced than children from two-parent homes. It's not hard to see how our numbers will continue to grow.

But it's not just a statistical predisposition for divorce that we children of divorce carry with us. Studies are constantly predicting all the trouble we'll be getting into. The Centers for Disease Control gets into the act with its July 2002 issue of the journal *Vital and Health Statistics,* which shows that we are more likely to "drop out of high school, have lower grades and attendance while in school . . . (and) become single parents than those raised in two-parent families." We also tend to fare worse than our counterparts from intact families in terms of depression, alcohol and drug abuse, and getting ourselves arrested. And then there are all those factors that cannot be measured. Like how we feel when someone professes their love to us, when we are alone in our beds at night, or when we move alone from one city to another.

I remember in graduate school talking to another writer who was, like me, obsessed with the lives of grown children of divorce. "As far as I'm concerned," she said emphatically, "there are two camps of people. Those of us who have lived through our world being ripped in two and those who haven't. Those who haven't can try, but I don't think they can ever understand how ill at ease we are, how we are always waiting for the other shoe to drop, for the dreaded bad news to arrive." At the time I thought maybe she was making too sharp a distinction, but lately I've been thinking maybe not.

The malaise of spirit that haunts adult children of divorce has been the subject of poetry, films, and novels as well as so-cial studies. The coke-snorting kids from *Less Than Zero* were from fractured families, as was the potential-wasting charac-ter played by Winona Ryder in *Reality Bites,* who, despite brains and beauty, was unable to commit to a steady course in either work or love. For *The Love They Lost: Living with the Legacy of Our Parents' Divorce,* author Stephanie Stall inter-viewed 120 adult children of divorce as she sought to define this emotional landscape. Writing about her own experi-ence, she eloquently describes the trepidation that plagues many adult children of divorce, "Only recently have I been able to connect the dots in my mind, to clearly see how the fact that I stumble over the words 'I love you' travels a straight path back to a childhood where I witnessed love be-trayed, how the sudden dips of melancholy are recesses carved long ago." In *Split: Stories from a Generation Raised on Divorce,* a dozen or so young writers describe the fragmented despair of a generation raised on MTV, Kentucky Fried Chicken, and divorce. In her essay "California Overboard," Paula Gilovich

portrays her family's divorce as very much rooted in a specific cultural moment (the Reagan eighties) and a specific
place (the Silicon Valley):

> *All of my California friends with their California parents*
> *and their California divorces dreamed of their parents*
> *getting back together. They dreamed of reconciliation on*
> *the eve of adulthood. They had infantile habits that*
> *seemed to accompany their fairytale cravings: still wet-*
> *ting beds at twelve, sucking thumbs at sixteen unable to*
> *sleep with the lights off even after graduation.*

I do think there is an angst particular to those of us who
grew up in a divided universe, and I'm certain that there are
a great many activities that cause us a good deal more neurosis than they should, from managing our time and anxiety
during exam week to saying "I do," to charting the arcs of
our careers and personal lives. But I also have a hunch that
there are a host of positive qualities common to us that never
get named. Perhaps we are more resilient and less gullible
than your average bear. Maybe we're good at keeping going
even with chaos ensuing all around us. Do we tend to enter
relationships with a complete and utter respect for their ulti-
mate frailty? Are we the friends you know you can call on
the darkest afternoon of your life because you know that we
will "get it"? And because you know, you just *know* we're not
going to say, "C'mon, it's not that bad."

· · ·

THE SEMINAR IS CALLED "WHAT ABOUT THE CHILDREN?" and is required of all parents of minor children seeking a divorce in King County. Even the title makes me feel guilty, dirty, and criminal, as though I'm headed to Monday-morning driving school to wipe Saturday night's DUI off my record. A couple of years ago, I was thinking of myself as the woman who had it all—a wife, the mother of two amazing daughters, an emerging writer—and now here I am, a single, unemployed mother lumbering into a court-ordered parent-ed class.

As we shuffle into the courthouse classroom, our private lives now in the hands of King County, a sunny, round-faced social worker hands us a booklet the color of a Crayola periwinkle crayon. On the front cover is a five-year-old's drawing of three stick figures—a mommy, daddy, and girl child—all smiling under the requisite sun. The sun's rays, as stumpy as building blocks, jut perilously close to Daddy's head. In a child's handwriting, blazing across the top of the page, are the words "Parents Still Love You When They Get Divorced." It occurs to me that at some moment in time, a real child must have sat down to create this disturbing portrait of the exhaustive lengths children will go to in order to make everything okay for their parents, even when their parents can't make everything okay for them. Perhaps it was even a contest. Draw your best picture of what it feels like to have your parents divorce!

I did not want to come here this morning. Did not want to sit in a room of troubled men and women who've messed up their children's lives. Did not want to hear sordid details, to hear about that son of a bitch who hasn't given her a cent for the kids since he ran out of their lives. And I did not want to count myself among the company of the woman in acid-washed jeans who perpetually has her hand up, who tells us that she and her ex had a good relationship "until crystal meth got in the picture."

But this class is mandatory for all divorcing parents. And it's not what I imagined as I took the bus downtown this morning to the King County Courthouse; I pictured myself as somehow exempt. I was the woman from the neighborhood of fleece jackets and free-range chickens who's "evolved," who's committed to the "good divorce," who's not really like all the other divorcing parents in the room. But now I realize I'm just as much a part of this as everyone else here who imagined not long ago that they, too, were better than this. I'm beginning to see us as a United Nations of divorcing parents, like we might all begin swaying shoulder-to-shoulder, singing "We Are the World." A big, teary world. I have to admit that this is actually the first time in months I've felt like I am among my own kind.

In my row of folding chairs, there is a strawberry blond woman whose red-rimmed eyes suggest that she hasn't stopped crying for more than five minutes in weeks, and a New Agey–looking Asian woman in a long batik caftan, and a petite Indian woman. When I laugh for a couple of beats too long after the narrator of the introductory video tells us that we may now be feeling "paranoid," but then concedes that in this case "someone may well be out to get you," the Indian woman smiles at me with understanding. She is the only one in our row who doesn't wipe her eyes at least once during the video on the psychological terrors a court-litigated custody dispute would inevitably evoke in our children. When the Asian woman cries, she takes off her glasses and rubs her whole face with her hands like a cat washing its face with balled-up paws.

The Asian woman tells the class that she is selling herbal medicines and that if any of us are interested, she will be available to talk after class. I consider this briefly—I'm very open these days to the idea of being sedated—but decide that it's probably not safe to mix the herbs with the prescription sleeping medication to which I am no doubt becoming addicted.

"I did not sleep four months!" she tells us, wagging four fingers at us emphatically. Many of us nod vigorously as she speaks, affirming what people outside of this room might not be able to: she is not exaggerating. It really was four months and it really is this bad.

There's one ten-minute break that won't get you anywhere near coffee or food, so I resign myself to a trip to the women's restroom, where I wait listlessly for my turn to pee. After the break, we are asked to get in groups to share our experiences, and my spine stiffens. I think of bolting, but then remember that the signed and notarized certificate I need to give the judge is snug in the facilitator's briefcase and won't be mine until I've endured every minute of this.

I mutter in my head something about this twisted New Age fascism that forces people to share feelings. What would George Orwell say? But still I'm up and scraping my metal chair along the floor, prepared to go where I must.

"Move into the group that matches your child's age," the facilitator sings out, as if she's dividing us up for a game of charades. "Infants to toddlers over here. Parents of three-to-six-year-olds in the middle of the room. Grade-school-age children to the right. And in the back of the room those lucky parents with teens."

I stand momentarily paralyzed and then ask, "What if you have a child in two different groups?"

"Well, then you'll need to make a choice. Maybe you could think about which of your children seems to be struggling more."

I quickly fast-forward through a filmstrip of the last few months with my kids—Jess with her few words about the divorce, but strange, locked-in afternoons when I can't tempt her out of her fantasy life; Natalie with her anger, her probing questions, her sudden mistrust of me. Now this whole thing seems like some kind of *Sophie's Choice* of a workshop, but I trudge toward the group that corresponds to Natalie's age, the guilt about Jess lingering around me like a cloud.

We drag our folding chairs into a jagged shape resembling a circle. Like the other groups, ours moves with the alacrity and vigor you'd associate with a group of inmates serving twenty to life. Finally we settle: two women—an affluent-looking African-American woman dressed in an elegant peach suit and me—and three men. The men's contingent includes two blue-collar guys with their arms folded across their chests and an Indian man with a pocket protector and a detached demeanor that shouts Boeing engineer.

The engineer immediately takes charge of our group, offering in his crisp Indian accent, "Shall we begin? Who would like to start?"

We are silent. Shame is the common denominator of our group; we mostly have our heads down, casting sidelong glances at a neighbor's running shoe tracing circles on the linoleum floor. Beyond the shame, I am pretty sure there is an electric current of mistrust traveling through our crooked little circuit, and it is a very particular one. The men don't trust us, and we don't trust them. Even though we've never seen one another before today, all the men in the group are my soon-to-be-ex–husband, and I'm pretty sure that I and the woman beside me are their wives, their tired blond heads no doubt transposed over ours. We trust one another with our feelings no more than we'd trust a cat to babysit a mouse.

Finally the other woman clears her throat, and a palpable feeling of relief moves through the group. "I'm having a lot of trouble with my son," she says. And with those words, there is a shift: heads rise up a bit, legs uncross, the Boeing guy leans forward, and a few of us even dare to look her in the eye. We are all having trouble with our kids. For some of us the trouble is terrible.

"He's so angry, but he won't talk to me and he won't talk

to his father," she says. One of the blue-collar men swallows hard, and the other one shifts his gaze toward her as she tells us all the things we already know about our own kids, the things we know but haven't admitted to ourselves: how they shut themselves away for a while, sometimes a good long while, and you can bang on their doors and their windows, but they won't let you in until they're good and ready. And there's really not all that much you can do about it.

It's one of those holy moments when someone says the truth, and everyone's defenses begin to melt. It is real and undeniable and each of us is affected in our own way. We remember briefly the startling humanity of one another. But in a flash the moment passes. The facilitator of the group calls us back to order, and we look at one another in bewilderment, and just like that it is over. The same force that corralled us together is pulling us apart. The connection we so fleetingly felt breaks into molecules and dissipates into the fluorescent air of the windowless room. We are up and dragging our folding chairs behind us once again, settling back into our places, getting ready to face whatever will come next.

Part Two

Adjustment

Faith is the bird that sings
when the dawn is still dark.

—RABINDRANATH TAGORE

7

The Sound of One Hand Clapping

Let me come clean right away and say this: my mom helped me with money. Quite a bit.

If she hadn't, I wouldn't be able to write that she helped me because I'd be at Starbucks pouring espresso shots into paper cups. I know you're thinking kindly, *Oh, you'd have a better job than that*. Don't be so sure.

I began a strenuous but halfhearted job search almost immediately after the split, even though in my heart I believed our life as a family would implode if I were to attempt full-time work. My daughters were attending two different schools with two sets of start and stop times. One of the schools, twenty minutes from our house, had no bus service. Jessie was participating in a physical therapy program that was offered at only one location in Seattle, a forty-minute drive away. Natalie's schedule was packed with school, dance, and Girl Scouts. When we weren't darting around the city, we were shopping for dinner, cooking dinner, eating dinner, cleaning up from dinner, or helping the third-grade class build a replica of a Seattle neighborhood. And yes, sometimes I was lying facedown on my king-size bed hissing one-word questions like "How?" and "Why?" into the pillow. And that takes time, too.

Two competing forces were gathering within me like generals commanding little armies—one a dress-for-successer in pumps, hell-bent on securing a high-paying job with benefits *now,* and the other a sort of hippie chick who sighed and said things like, "Doesn't it actually end up costing more to work than stay home?" Maybe it was the post-divorce identity crisis. One day I'd be enmeshed in a sort of *Working Girl* meets *Kramer vs. Kramer* fantasy that this divorce was somehow going to catapult me into a new high-voltage career that I could never have foreseen. The next, I'd champion the simple life—extolling the virtues of walking to school, growing our veggies in the backyard, and declaring a moratorium on restaurant meals.

Maybe it was the brutal reality of looking for a job after more than a handful of years on the mommy track that made me so confused. In the short term, it was the hippie who won out. She insisted that the way to go was to spend as little money as humanly possible, stay home and make food for the children, and keep life calm. And that was how the first year after the split did come to pass, and some days I accepted it, but most days I still let the woman in pumps drive me to the computer to scan the want ads, fill out mountains of online applications, and write an endless number of cover letters designed to drive my square peg into whatever round hole was open that day. The truth was, though, no matter how much money I could save by cutting back here and there, I still needed more income.

At the nadir of all this, a friend who worked for Microsoft e-mailed me about an opening in his department—recruiting. Recruiting? Why, I was *made* for that. Of course, *recruiting!* Why hadn't I thought of it before? Recruiting was *it*. As it turned out, the job didn't actually involve recruiting, however. It was actually a scheduling position that involved spending one's day nailed to Microsoft Outlook, juggling the schedules of scores of moving objects. It also didn't pay that well. And it was a contract position. But it offered that commodity for which souls are bought and sold: amazing benefits.

A few of my friends from grad school worked at Microsoft, and they spent the next few days with me on the phone grooming me for the notorious Microsoft interview, known for poking at the inner reaches of your psyche until at last you lie prone before them, bare and completely unfurled. Microsoft interviewers are famous for the hypothetical question, sort of the corporate version of the Buddhist koan. You're in a room with no windows and you can't go outside, how can you determine the weather? You need to make toast but you have no toaster, what do you do? Why is a manhole cover round? What is the sound of one hand clapping?

This is exactly the sort of question that stumps me,

especially in an interview situation. I'm likely to just panic and spit out something like "So don't have toast, have a bagel." But in a few short days, my friends were able to cram into my head the sort of "outside the box" thinking that apparently made a person desirable in the eyes of the region's largest employer. My friends also told me that the big push right now—after the burnout workaholic nineties—was to hire *balanced* employees, tortoises that could keep plugging away for the long haul, still producing and delivering long after the flaccid bodies of exhausted hares have lined the sides of the road.

So, after an initial phone interview with the temp agency, the day of the real interview—I should say *interviews*—arrives. After lounging about in the airtight waiting area for a good half hour with some twenty-four-year-old programmers, my day is explained to me. There will be a number of interviews—how many the receptionist cannot say—one after another. After each interview, I will be brought back to the waiting area and told the time of the next interview and the name of the interviewer. Okay.

The first interviewer is twenty-five and wearing what I'm sure *Glamour* magazine would deem "inappropriate office wear": lace-up boots, a miniskirt, and a semitransparent peasant blouse. I sail through this one. She tells me after each question how great I've done, and like a seal, I gulp the fish greedily and give her the next answer.

But as the day wears on and more-senior people conduct the interviews, the dreaded questions begin to arrive, posed by increasingly serious and better-dressed recruiters. Just before lunch, I'm asked by a forty-year-old in a red blazer, "What about contract work appeals to you?"

I'm certain there's no viable way to answer this question. Maybe the lack of benefits and real salary, I think to myself. Or maybe it's something more intangible—the edginess of not knowing from one day to the next where you stand. But I have to come up with a real answer, and then I think, Well, maybe it's because I'm returning to work after being at home with the kids, but then I think, No, that's too soccer-mom. It's way too lightweight to mention the kids. I'm starting to sweat and then suddenly I'm channeling a savvier friend when I blurt out, "I've always wanted to work at Microsoft, and I thought a contract position would be a great way to see where I fit in and learn more about the company and its needs."

By right after lunch, I start to see a pattern emerging that is making me more than nervous. I can tell I'm doing well, and at times I tell myself I'm a shoo-in, but as my confidence rises, so does my sense that I am applying for the most miserable job on earth. Each interview begins with either "How do you deal with frustration?" or "Describe a situation in which you've dealt with competing demands." A typical follow-up question is, "How would you feel if you spent the whole morning setting up a schedule, only to find that everything you've done is predicated on the participation of a manager who will actually be out of town that day?" Hey, I'm thinking, where's my toaster question?

By four in the afternoon, I'm completely worn down. I am increasingly aware that there is no natural air or light in the building, and I feel my tongue swelling and have the sense that I may begin panting any moment. I'm also a little slap-happy. I feel like I would say anything just to get out of the building and go home. I guess they have me just where they want me.

Interviewer number five is an Asian woman about my age in a brightly colored, hand-knit sweater. I'm completely obsessed, by now, with how divergent the manner of dress is in this office. I almost want to stay to see what costume the next player will wear. She asks me, as they all must, "What about contract work appeals to you?"

I can barely see or hear at this point. The fluorescent light has broken all the images in the room down to tiny pixels that jump out at me and then recede into the fuzzy background. I almost say, "A manhole cover is round so it can't fall into the hole," but at the last minute I swerve, and in my delirium, I hear myself say, "I'm just returning to the workforce after being home with my kids. I thought a contract position might be the way to ease into the workplace. Not that I think the position will be 'easy' per se—"

"You have kids?" she breaks in.

"Two daughters." There, it's out. I'm just a mommy looking for something to do while the kids are in school. Ideally, I should be hosting Tupperware parties or selling Mary Kay to the ladies from my step aerobics class.

"We're all moms in this group!" she says, like I've just joined the cheerleading squad. "It's great. We really work together! How old are your daughters?"

"Five and nine," I answer, still cautious.

"I have a nine-year-old!" She says this like she's just realized that we're both Irish step-dancing champions from Fargo, North Dakota.

"Boy or girl?" I ask, my confidence growing.

"Girl."

"Hannah Montana?" I ask, issuing the password that grants entrance into the kingdom of tween-girl pop culture.

"*That's So Raven,*" she coos back, and that's it. I'm in.

We're still laughing as she turns back to her questions. "So, I'm sure you're used to frustration?"

"I'm majoring in it," I say, and again we both giggle.

"And flexible?" she says with a wave of the note cards, as if to say why do we even bother with this formality. "I'm sure your work at home requires you to go with the flow."

I cringe a little, thinking of all the times lately the kids have witnessed me shouting, stamping my feet, and cursing into the washing machine. But I push those images aside and say, "That's the thing about being a mom. You have to be able to work with multiple schedules that are constantly in flux. If you lose it, so does everyone else, so you just have to be calm."

"This position is actually a *lot* like motherhood," she says.

I smile, thinking, That explains the low wage and why all

the people who work in this office are women. It seems very doubtful that I, given the challenge I've had managing life with two children, could actually sustain a work life that is "like motherhood" while handling *actual* motherhood single-handedly at home. Despite everything I have said today, I am not flexible and I do not "go with the flow."

"Now," she says, clearing her throat, the mood shifting back to somber as she turns back to her notes, "let's take a hypothetical situation."

Ah, I'm thinking, I've made it to the hypotheticals.

"It's five o'clock," she begins, twirling her pencil, looking up to the ceiling as she falls into the soothing reverie of constructing a hypothetical. "You've got a personal emergency at home—perhaps one of your daughters has accrued a minor injury," she adds, pointing the pencil's tip at me briefly before continuing. "And all your coworkers have left for the day. Suddenly you get a call from another department that a situation has come up that needs our immediate attention. What would you do?"

Okay, the hypotheticals. Here we go. Okay! Think! What the hell? One of my kids is hurt? I'm out of here. But that's the worst answer. But wait. Balance, remember? They're looking for balance. They're not looking for crazy nuts who want hurt kids separated from their mothers. This woman is a mother. If her daughter were hurt, she'd be out of here in a flash.

"I'd work with the person for a few minutes on the phone to see how we could bandage the situation for the day, and then plan to be here first thing in the morning and reschedule whatever it is for then. There are few things that can't wait until the next morning," I say, sounding either balanced or insane.

"Okay," she says flatly, in no way indicating whether this is a good answer or not. "Same thing. Same situation. But this time it's Bill Gates's office calling."

Okay, in real life, there's a chance that I might treat a person of enormous wealth and power with more deference than the woman down the hall in HR, but this is Interview World and, if only to save face, if only to somehow *win* (although win *what,* I no longer know), I must give not the real answer but the *right* answer. I consider two options: either you work with Bill's office or you don't. If there's a third, I'm not smart enough to think of it. So your choices are to say that you'd risk your job by being the idiot who tells Bill Gates's office you're needed at home to treat a minor flesh wound, or to be exposed as the fawning panderer that you truly are.

I take a breath. "Okay, same answer."

"Same answer as before?" she asks in the even voice of a game-show host asking, "Final answer?"

"Yes," I say and she smiles—genuinely?—at me. Perhaps they've had trouble in the past with fawning panderers.

She ushers me out of the room and into the lobby where I've been deposited by each of the preceding interviewers, and vanishes. I look blankly at the receptionist, who says, "That's it. You're done."

I stumble out of the building, back into light and air, and

try to remember who I was six hours earlier. Did I drive here? Is there someone I should phone right now to say I'm back on the planet? I find my car. I pick up the kids. Somehow I make it home.

The next day I hear from the temp agency. Apparently I did great. All the interviewers with the choice of "hire" or "don't hire" assigned me as a "hire." They have only one more person to interview, but she doesn't see any reason why it's not going to work out. I hang up the phone. Do I want to work in a job where smiling in the face of frustration is the crowning achievement of the day? Do I want to work somewhere with no natural air or light? Do I want to commute while my kids whittle away their lives in costly extended-day programs? No, no, and hell no. But I'm not really in a position to say no.

I've resigned myself to the job and its frustration, and start going through my closet trying to figure out how I might leave the house *every day* looking somewhat ready for work. But I don't hear back the next day, and I don't hear anything the day after that either. After four days, I e-mail the woman at the temp agency again, and she e-mails back, "They have decided on another candidate. They may have another position and I will find out if you're being considered for it. I know that they liked you and you got great feedback. I will let you know what I hear!"

I'm disappointed in the sense that I entered a contest and was defeated, but I'm also relieved. I won't be asked to ac-

commodate the impossible. I won't be asked to choose between Bill Gates's office and a hurt child at home.

The thing is, I don't think it really matters what you say
in an interview. You can say all the right things, but people
can still feel who you really are; they sense your limitations,
your hesitations, and your inner hippie chick. Even if they're
not conscious of this information, they still intuit on some
level what you can and cannot do. At least some people can.
At least, I think, these people did.

FOR NOW, I STILL HAVE MY PART-TIME TEACHING POSITION
at UW to keep a little money drizzling in. I've been teaching
creative writing classes there on and off since Jess was born,
and now I'm grateful that I have not only a small source of
income, but also a place where I must show up with a coher-
ent mind and brushed teeth. For a few hours each week,
teaching offers me a reprieve from my own thoughts. In the
classroom, all worries are scorched from my mind, and I'm
transported to a place where the novel or the student story
we're discussing is the only matter of concern.

It's a rainy November afternoon, and I'm sitting in my
shabby little part-time office at the university, waiting out
the eternal office hour that students rarely use, when Kathy
calls me. We aren't too far past Halloween, and she's ready
to start talking about Christmas.

"I'm thinking of canceling Christmas this year," I say. I

look out the window to the parking lot of the Husky Union Building where students stream into the building in pairs and clusters for their afternoon break. I imagine that they all have parents somewhere with ski cabins and time-shares and soon they'll all be jetting off to be ensconced in the privilege of being upper middle class—old enough to be on their own, but young enough to be flown home and given presents off their Amazon wish lists.

"I was thinking the three of you could come down here," my sister says.

I grunt a low sound, maybe even a moan. I'm sure it would be easier for the three of us to go on an Arctic expedition than to get ourselves and our Christmas down to the far reaches of New Mexico.

"I know what you're thinking," she says. "You're thinking it's too much money. But I don't want you to worry about that. We'll take care of the tickets."

I want to say that I'm too tired to go to the library, let alone make connecting flights with young children still acting out their anger about their parents' separation, but I feel like I'm too tired to tell her that I'm too tired. I don't think anyone has ever successfully denied my sister. She's like the police, the God of the Old Testament, and Barbra Streisand all rolled into one. No is not an option.

"I tell you what," she says, "Christmas is coming no matter what you do, and if you don't make plans you'll be sitting there in December with the babies up in the gray rain, wishing you were anywhere but there."

Only my sister could make me feel both deeply cared for and unequivocally threatened at the same time. "I'll think about it," I say, and just then a student pops his head in my door. "Gotta go," I say.

"Book the tickets!" I hear her commanding just as the receiver reaches its cradle.

LATELY I'VE BEEN ASKING KATHY WHAT SHE REMEMBERS about our parents' divorce and her move to Mexico. Partly I'm trying to figure out Natalie's perspective on the split, and partly I'm feeling increasingly as though I must find some sort of logic in the seemingly random events that followed my parents' divorce. Maybe if I can make sense of the original chaos I was born into, I can begin to decode the scrambled life I'm living now.

My elaborate scene of my father coming and taking Kathy from our apartment, born out of one stray comment from my father, probably has no foundation. Kathy remembers going for a visit to JoJo's house, the pink stucco bungalow in Redwood City with the Rangpur lime tree beside the back door. It was night. She was asleep in the drafting room with the giant loom and the single bed, the room we kids stayed in when we slept the night at JoJo's house. Dad came to get her. He woke her and took her to the car. They drove north in the dark to his cabin in the Sierra Nevada foothills and a few weeks later south to Mexico. She didn't know, she tells me now, that she was leaving forever the apartment where she lived briefly with our mother, my sister, Susan, and me. She never, as far as she knows, said the word *good-bye*. In the story she tells me, there is no good-bye scene, just a slow dissolve from one setting to the next. A gray fade-out.

Two days before Christmas, the three of us are flying above Midland, Texas, a little spot of light in a sea of black flat land. Oil rigs, like creatures from another planet, bob their heads mechanically up and down along the lunar landscape. All I can think as we land is, How could this bleak terrain have spawned a president? and This is the town in which the radio stations will no longer play the Dixie Chicks. Not the Sex Pistols, mind you, but the *Dixie* Chicks.

A few hours later and a truck ride down an infinite dirt road, we're in Hobbs, New Mexico, in my sister's house, which I think of as "the moon station." Outside the house, tumbleweeds the size of cattle trot aimlessly down the desolate street. Once every few minutes, the wind picks up a cloud of dust and the sky turns instantly from blue to brown. The phrase "inhospitable to life-forms" runs through my head each time I look out the window. I try taking the kids for a walk a couple of times, but the wind blows a steady stream of dirt into our eyes and mouths.

We stay inside, hermetically sealed in our moon station. My sister's house is nothing like mine. When you shut one of her doors, you can hear the hiss of the house sealing vacuum-tight like Tupperware. In my house, there is no chance of dying of carbon monoxide poisoning; you can nearly slide a hand between the bottom edge of the front door and the weather-stripping. My house is a hundred years old, and some of the dirt on the kitchen windows dates back that far. Kathy has a team of housekeepers. You can open her fridge and identify things you could actually eat, not just balls of tinfoil wrapped around leftovers, and dried-out orange cheese someone forgot to wrap up, and ancient jars of poppyseed salad dressing.

Over the last few months my eyes have opened to problems with my house that I somehow, inexplicably, didn't notice in the last few years of my marriage. The following is an incomplete list of the house's problems that have just begun to pop into my consciousness:

1. There's one hall cupboard that has to be opened with a fork. I'm actually proud of the fact that I've permanently attached this fork to the bare screw where the knob is missing, so that when I want to open the cupboard I merely have to pull on the fork rather than fetching a fork, attaching the fork, and *then* yanking open the cupboard door.

2. The laurel hedge that surrounds our house is now beyond human pruning capabilities. It's more than twenty-five feet tall in spots and a haven for all sorts of wildlife. The neighborhood tomcats can often be spotted prowling under the canopy of the hedge, their bodies taut with anticipation, and swaggering out later, licking their chops

and adjusting their belt buckles. Things go *on* in there. Animal things I tell myself not to think about.

3. The wallpaper upstairs is peeling and curling in on itself in a manner that would be very appealing in the bark of a birch tree.

4. There is no light fixture in the master bedroom upstairs— just two bare bulbs shining. A year ago, Kevin accidentally shattered the fixture in the process of shaking out the bedspread. I said something nastily to him about which one of us was going to go to the store to replace the fixture, and he answered snidely that of course he would do it, and then I held out to see how long it would take him to do it. Proving what? I don't know.

5. My office has a pull-chain light that relies a tad too heavily on the use of the opposable thumb and forefinger. The chain is in fact no longer a chain, just a nubbin of string that one has to fish out, secure between thumb and pointer finger, and then pull with the utmost care so that the nubbin doesn't slip away and retreat into its hiding hole.

6. The bathroom floor has gaps that allow water to drip directly onto the moldy carpet in the basement, which is filled with everything I haven't wanted to deal with over the last four years. Oscillating fan no longer oscillates? Pop it in the basement. Box of scratched CDs? Down the stairs it goes. If you wanted to, you could conduct an archaeological household project, determining the date

of each discarded object's descent to this wasteland by measuring its proximity to the basement stairs.

Here in Kathy's house, there are two satellite dishes on the roof, a TV in every room, and a big-screen TV in the living room. Natalie and Jess are quite content to spend the entire holiday picking up satellite signals from every corner of the country and sucking back hours of Nick Jr. The fridge is stocked with endless sandwich meats and diet drinks. I no longer worry about whether or not it's good for the kids to watch so much TV. We're visiting another culture and must temporarily suspend any prior sense of how things should be. We munch salty chips and sandwiches with our icy drinks in front of the big screen and fall headlong into the same episodes of *Bewitched* and *I Dream of Jeannie* I watched as a child. Life as we know it no longer exists. Time and money are of no consequence. I'm neither married nor unmarried. I'm one step away from living in a genie bottle, lounging on pillows in harem pants, and calling a cute astronaut "Master."

Sleeping in one of the guest rooms with the kids, I feel like a child myself, as though in losing a husband I've lost some status in my family as well as in the world. I think sulkily about how a couple would always get their own room, but an insignificant single mother, you can just stick her in that big old bed with her kids and then they'll have her on tap twenty-four hours a day and trample any of her remaining personal boundaries. I know this isn't rational. It's the only logical sleeping arrangement, given all the other guests in the house, but still I lie awake and aggravated, listening to the heater's endless cycle of kicking on and then shutting down, watching the numbers on the clock, thinking how I never wanted to be a single mother. I wanted to be a married mother.

Earlier in the evening, I pulled Kathy into her walk-in closet to rant and rave about how angry I am.

"I fucking hate my fucking life," I said into a rack of blazers of every color.

"I know you do," she said. One of the things I love most about my sister is that she's not afraid of the truth. You can tell her anything and she won't flinch. She's talked dozens of people out of suicide. She's a card-carrying member of TAHN, the Texas Association of Hostage Negotiators. She lived by her own wits in a foreign country before she'd even reached puberty. A little garden-variety emotional agony doesn't scare her one bit.

"You're not going to talk me out of it? You're a psychologist, aren't you supposed to talk me out of it?"

"First, we affirm," she said. "Then we talk you out of it when you're not looking."

"Can we just skip to that part?" I said, staring at the boxes and boxes of shoes lined on the shelf above me, each with the side of the box with the little penciled image of the shoe facing outward.

"In a year, maybe two, you'll feel better."

"A year, maybe two? I do not fucking accept that. It's like I've been in a car wreck or something."

My brother-in-law knocked on the closet door just then and said, "Kathy, you need to get out here and cut the roast."

"Okay, just a minute," she said, and I heard his steps muffled by thick carpeting as he walked away. I looked at all the nice slippery dry-cleaning bags and thought maybe I could just suffocate myself in them and skip dinner.

Kathy hugged me long and hard. "I know this is tough, girl, but it is going to get easier. You'll see. Give it time."

Staring at the ceiling above the bed now, I try to cheer myself with a round of "Surely, being single must have some advantages!" Failing at that, I switch to one of my favorites from home, "This is *your* life now. You can do whatever you want!" Usually this ends with a resounding, "But there's nothing I want to do! And it's not *my* life; it's *their* life. I can't do whatever I want. I need to take care of them." But this time my mind catches hold of a hazy image.

It starts with just a color—a creamy lavender, Natalie's favorite. Next, beside it, I see a splash of super girly pink, the color I associate with Jess, who's still deeply entrenched in the Barbie years. I see myself walking up the stairs in our house, past our curling wallpaper, to the master bedroom on my left and the tiny office on my right. I always held on tight to that office while Kevin and I were married. It was the only space in the house that was mine. But now imagine that little room is awash in cotton-candy pink, and that across the hall, a tremendous field of lavender, iridescent and shining, stands where the master bedroom once was.

I sit up in bed. I remember that Kevin will have the girls all next week, a week I've been dreading. But now I'm thinking that I could use that time to secretly rearrange the house. I could move myself from the two rooms upstairs and make their bedroom on the main floor my bedroom/office. I'm alone now. It doesn't matter if I work in the room I sleep in. Then I'll paint their rooms and move all their stuff in before they come home. Natalie has wanted her own room for years. She and Jess are constantly involved in territorial skirmishes that end, at best, in irritated détentes.

I could make Natalie happy.

I could make Jess happy.

I could give them something they once thought impossible, something that might begin the new year with hope.

8

And the Wisdom to Know the Difference

I see her at a distance, and I am once again the girl with the floppy socks drooping down her ankles. She strides over to me in a few easy steps. She is, after all, six feet tall. Her name is Greta, but in my mind she will always be The Viking. She's the only mom I know who wears a blazer with her jeans and somehow makes that seem just right, not silly or overdressed. She's also one of the few women I've ever met who gets away with trading almost no social niceties. If you say to her, "Nice jacket," she murmurs a very short "Mm-hmm" and then quickly asks whether you've had a chance to read the school's new mission statement, which of course I never have. I probably wouldn't read it at the best of times. Even at the very tiptop of my game, I wouldn't be able to keep up with this woman, and now the futility of trying strikes me with tsunami force.

"I'm so glad I ran into you. This gives us some face time," she says.

Face time? Then I realize it's one of those Microsoft phrases; instead of e-mailing, we're going to have some luxurious face time. Greta used to be in marketing at Microsoft, and from what I gather she's now retired (well before the golden years) and devotes herself indefatigably to committee work for worthy causes and philanthropic endeavors. I wonder briefly if she could take *me* on as a cause, but I know she sees me—and this is what endears me to her—as an equal.

"I want to get you in the loop on some things," she says with great earnestness. The loop is a place the Microsoft people spend a lot of time inside of. My loop these days is the well-worn path between my kitchen and my bed.

As she speaks, a realization is gathering inside me and there is a tightening in my stomach. I'm beginning to remember vaguely the e-mails about an auction committee that started arriving from her in the first foggy days after Kevin and I split up. I clicked on one once and quickly closed it, just catching the phrase "brainstorm ideas for the coming auction." I checked to see whether it was addressed to a large group or just to me. Just to me, it was.

"It's great we're going to have a chance to work together. I'm glad you signed up for the auction committee this year," she says.

Signed up? I *know* I did not sign up for any such thing. Could I have forgotten? There's no way I'd sign up for the

auction committee and then forget. That would be like failing to remember you'd enlisted in the military. As she talks
on about generating ideas for a class project for the auction,
I search my mind like a Kafka character for some clue to how
I've fallen into this murky labyrinth. I can just barely make
out an image of a sign-up sheet during the Open House the
first week of school. It had been placed on the overhead pro-
jector, and I'd scanned it upside down and searched for the
most contained assignment. I'd chosen one that I knew
would be limited to one day of preparation and would involve no lengthy philosophical debates or open-ended tasks:
the Valentine's Day party. I'd written my name under that.
Or *had* I?

"The sign-up sheet," I blurt.

"Pardon?"

"Oh, nothing," I say, but I realize now that my haste had
been my undoing. Anxious to secure the easy Valentine's
party gig, I'd jotted down my name before I could get the
sheet right side up in front of me and had inadvertently
signed up for the most ill-defined and interminable of assignments—the class auction project. Oh, no!

"So, I think we should meet as soon as possible. I've col-
lected some data and I'd like to get together and bounce
some ideas off you."

This is my chance. I either get out of it right here and
now, or I accept the fact that I will be spending part of the
next few months doing something I don't want to do. Already mired in misery and self-pity over my finances, I hesi-

tate to think that spurring on children to create auction items for a school to which some parents routinely donate an extra ten grand on top of their hefty tuition bill is the most obvious route to good cheer. I look at Greta, her face so open and expectant, so oblivious of the apathy that courses through the veins of the person before her. There is an innocence about her I feel compelled to protect. Her belief in our little school is tremendous, almost more than its old brick walls can hold. I saw her once a few years back in a parent-ed discussion about parenting values. She was leaning forward at a sharp angle to hear another parent speak, her blue eyes focused intently on the speaker as if nothing in the world could be more interesting, as if the sheer force of her attention could transform the world into a better place, like the guy on TV who used to bend spoons with just his thoughts.

"So when's a good time for you?" I ask her, and it is done. I'm climbing aboard the Viking ship.

Within a few weeks we decide we will help the children to make silk scarves for their mothers, which will be sold at the auction for a hundred dollars a pop. I have a searing sense of my own complicity with evil, as I know we will essentially be holding the parents attending the auction at gunpoint ("Dad, please buy the scarf I made for Mom tonight. *Please!*") for something that I cannot afford myself. Greta's unflinching belief in the school and the essential goodness of fund-raising keeps her safe from these thoughts, as does the fact that she functions in a remote currency market. On any given day her hundred dollars is worth to her roughly the equivalent of ten regular-person dollars.

Greta has absolutely no resistance to any idea, any task. She is the embodiment of the can-do attitude, in a way that I find intimidating but also intriguing. Maybe things aren't as hard as I make them out to be? Maybe I could adopt Greta's habit of nodding my head sharply and chirping "sure" or "absolutely" when people ask me if I can take on long, open-ended assignments like researching the materials needed to make scarves. Maybe if I could shake off just a little of my doubt and fear, I, too, could be bounding from one task to the next instead of curling into a ball for an afternoon nap.

We quickly agree to work on the projects at her house, both of us no doubt sensing that her house will be better equipped for wherever this project might take us. Her house was once selected as the site for a casual-sporty clothing company's Christmas catalog shoot. I guess some company rep just knocked on the door and said we love you, can we use your house? "It was a nightmare," her husband tells me. "We'd never do it again." I am just the type of reader the casual-sporty clothing marketers know they can conquer. With images of an armoire bathed in soft candlelight and an evergreen wreath adorning a hand-carved door, a woman like me can be rendered helpless, calling up the order hotline well after midnight, ordering polar fleeces, stretchy pants, and oh-so-casual sweaters in which to enjoy a hot toddy by the fire with friends who've also married well.

Each time I pull up in front of her house, I pause in the car and take a deep breath. It's like I'm entering some sort of cell where I'll have to face the worst of my jealousies, insecurities, and my gnawing sense of inferiority—something like Room 101 in Orwell's *1984*. A Buddhist professor of mine once told me that he did a meditation in which he chanted over and over, "All men are created equal," and this is exactly what I tell myself before I go into Greta's house, with its wraparound veranda, inboxes and outboxes labeled with her children's names, and her young retired husband with his laptop slung over his knee, firing up some new startup company in their well-appointed family room.

UNDER OUR BEDS ARE THE THINGS WE DON'T KNOW WHAT to do with and the things we don't want anyone to see. Under mine you'd find a collection of framed wedding photos, a nonfunctioning electric blanket, a handheld massager, and a stash of books—*Spiritual Divorce, Making Divorce Easier on Your Child, The Divorce Recovery Sourcebook,* and, most embarrassingly, *Chicken Soup for the Single's Soul,* a book I'd sandwiched between a few classics for the benefit of the scruffy twenty-two-year-old cashier who'd lethargically rung up my order.

In just about any bookstore, the two shelving areas perpetually in a state of disarray are the ones devoted to sex and to divorce. These are the subjects we desperately want to know more about and are equally desperate to distance ourselves from. One friend of mine—too squeamish to check out a library book on divorce—used to sit on the floor in the divorce section, systematically going through book after book, taking notes and plotting her way out of her life while her children played a few rows down in the children's section.

The book that's helped me the most is *Spiritual Divorce,* by Debbie Ford. Ford sees divorce as a "spiritual wake-up call," a chance to forgive ourselves and our spouses and move on to what she calls—and what I hope really *is*—an extraordinary life. By this time I've heard "And how *are* the kids doing?" so many times and read so many doomsaying articles about the fate of divorced children that this book is balm for my soul.

I'm aware that children of divorce often experience life-long repercussions from their parents' choices, and I'm doing everything I can to keep the playing field relatively level, to make sure this divorce goes as well as it can, and that they still respect their parents and still feel loved. But I also need to feel that It's Not the End of the World, to borrow the title of Judy Blume's preteen novel about divorce (which Natalie and I read together). Maybe we can still be really, really happy. Not just survive, but flourish. For so many years we were a fairly happy family, riding tandem bikes and hosting ice-skating parties. It seems too much of an identity shift to trudge into our futures with the word BROKEN flashing in neon above us. It seems too much to ask that I should feel lingering guilt about the quality of my children's family life when until recently we—both Kevin and I—were doing what we could to give them a joyful life that included lemonade stands, sleepovers, and parents who volunteered in the classroom every week.

Ford seems to think we can still be happy, and doesn't cite any statistics on high-school dropout rates for children of divorce, and because of this my loyalty to her and her book is unswerving. I may not read it in public, but I bring it out at night all the time and reread the most inspiring passages, reviewing in my mind to see if I've gone through the stages she outlines: Accept the situation for what it is—check; surrender to the situation—check; ask for divine guidance—check; accept responsibility for my life—not quite. I'm willing to work this sequence even though it reminds me not a small bit of the twelve steps of Alcoholics Anonymous. But that's okay. Redemption is my carrot.

In *Making Divorce Easier on Your Child*, Nicholas Long and Rex Forehand make a point that teeters between being too obvious to mention and so profound that judges should stamp it in red on every divorce decree: "As a person going through a divorce or who is divorced, it is important for you to realize that there are some things over which you have control and some things over which you have no control." This strikes me as sort of a Serenity Prayer for divorcing parents:

> *God grant me the serenity to accept that*
> *My ex-husband, whom I never could control,*
> *Is now way beyond conforming to my expectations,*

The courage to ask that child support arrive on time,
And the wisdom to know the difference.

Long and Forehand suggest, too, that divorcing parents recognize their "coping style" so they can realize when it is not working for them. The first style they identify is the "problem-focused style," in which you attempt to deal with a problem by changing or managing the situation so as to reduce stress. Next they describe an "emotion-focused style," in which you do not attempt to change the problem, but rather try to manage your emotional response to it. And finally they reveal the big bad boy: the avoidant coping style, in which you "attempt to cope with the stressor by denying its existence, refusing to deal with the situation, or perhaps resorting to alcohol, drugs or other ways of numbing your reaction to the situation."

All this makes me think of the various ways a person can react to a rundown house. You can make a list of what needs to be done and tackle the jobs one by one, or try to talk yourself out of your constant irritation over the flooding washing machine and peeling linoleum, or you could just pour yourself a big glass of pinot noir and pretend that those single-pane windows that can only be opened by an act of will and strength are part of your home's "old-world charm."

It occurs to me that the state of my house is a direct reflection of the state of my marriage in its final days. A great deterioration has occurred that I've been too busy or too preoccupied to notice. Or maybe I've just been too deter-mined *not* to notice. A saying runs through my head, "Show me your garden and I will tell ye who you are," and I imagine a possible correlate, "Show me the state of your home's re-pair and I will tell ye the state of your marriage." Is there a name for this special sort of denial about the state of dis-repair of a home? Do other people have this? Yes, they do, and some of them have toilets parked in their front yard and beat-up Chevys lining the driveway. My only advantage over them is that—so far—I've managed to keep most of my mess hidden inside.

I tend to waffle between the emotion-focused style and the avoidant one, which is really just a nicer way of saying "addict who doesn't want to deal with life." I'm no stranger to the phrase "It can't be done." When I was married, I relied on Kevin to tackle most of the larger, nastier tasks around the house. He has the sort of high-octane energy that made cleaning out a garage possible. I do not. I have the sort of energy that is good for wiping counters, checking e-mail, making one child's lunch (but not two), or reading one story to my children from the book titled *Five-Minute Bedtime Sto-ries*. (I've always found a certain remarkable baldness in this titling—I really cannot pretend that I am the good mother who is reading the school-endorsed twenty minutes a night with her child if I am reading one story from this book. If I read one small picture book, it may still take only five min-utes, but at least I have the option of pretending that it took longer.)

Mine is an ADD type of energy that enjoys tasks that can be taken from start to completion in about the amount of time it takes to smoke a cigarette, an average of seven minutes. The length of time, say, it might take a sixteen-year-old boy to make love to his girlfriend or to fold a medium load of laundry. I do not have the sort of energy that is required to toil at tasks I despise for periods longer than seven minutes. Of course, I have done tasks I despise for longer periods of time, but not without tantrumming or causing myself a huge amount of internal anguish.

One day I'm in the neighborhood grocery-slash-hardware store and it occurs to me that it would be possible to purchase a knob to replace the fork dangling from the hall cupboard. I feel a bit overwhelmed by the thought, but steer my cart over to the home hardware section of the store, thinking, How hard can it be? I stand in front of an array of knobs—stainless steel, brushed nickel, wood, ceramic, plastic posing as crystal—and think, So this is how it's done. From what I can tell, it looks as if homeowners have a problem or need and then go to the store—with a list, perhaps?—and buy the needed supplies. I look at the back of several knobs. I can see where the cupboard's currently bare screw, the one the fork is now holding on to for dear life, could be inserted. I feel a bit powerful and a bit afraid. I think maybe I should phone Kevin. "You know that missing knob in the hall?" I would say, "I'm here at the store and I'm about to replace it. Is that okay?"

I look at each of the knobs, feeling as if so much depends

on choosing the perfect one. In the end, I pick a ceramic one with a little blue heart painted on it. It seems just right.

NOW I HAVE MY LAVENDER AND PINK VISION AND A WEEK alone. Until now I've dreaded this week, feared the way the emptiness of the house would resound through the halls as it does on Kevin's Friday nights with the kids. But I'm filled with purpose and ready to fly into action. I get out the phone book and call a moving company, an electrician, and IKEA. Moving the girls from the one room they shared on the main floor to the two bedrooms upstairs is sort of like an algebra problem. It takes me a while to figure out the order of operations—move their stuff into the living room and then my stuff into their old room? Or vice versa? But I tell myself to just jump in and keep moving step by step until everything shakes into its new spot, hoping the moving guys will figure out most of it.

The movers break down the old bunk bed and store it in the garage, move the girls' furniture up from the main floor and into the centers of their new upstairs rooms and bring down my desk, dresser, and bed to my new pale pink room with a border of fairies in gossamer gowns. An electrician comes and installs new outlets and a light switch so that Jessie won't have to pull on the nubbin of string to turn her bedroom light on. When they all clear out, I jump in the car and head for IKEA to buy single beds, lamps, a new desk for Jess's room, and some curtains for Natalie's. Last night I debated briefly about spending a chunk of money when the future is still uncertain, but I quickly decided this is exactly what money is for.

I can hardly wait to see their faces. I love the idea of total surprise. I feel something like a butterfly caught in my rib cage. It's the joy of anticipation. For the first time in a long while, I'm looking forward to something.

On Day Two, my friend Trish shows up bearing spackle, a putty knife, an X-acto knife, and a jumbo roll of masking tape. We spend hours repairing the walls and taping up the peeling wallpaper, soon to be repainted for the zillionth time, and prepping the windows. As we work, we drink coffee and listen to Lauryn Hill singing about a place called Zion on Jessie's little CD player. Trish is a worker bee who knows that action speaks louder than words. She was at my house the morning I called the lawyer and my mother-in-law, and while I was telling these people all these things I didn't want to be true, she scrubbed down my stove. She didn't say a word; she just took the greasy beast apart and stripped off all the days of mess I'd left behind. I walked through the kitchen once in a while with the cordless phone up to my ear, and there was my friend doing the very right thing at the very moment it needed to be done.

The next day I paint Natalie's new room, the room I once shared with my husband. At first a lot of angry thoughts vie for position in my head, like commuters on a hot afternoon, waiting for a train to take them home. Why didn't we ever paint this room when we were together? Why is it the same dingy blue it was when we moved in four years ago? While he was wasting his time and our money, he could have been here with me, making things better. Why didn't he want to be with me? How could he have bailed out on us like that? I push the roller up and down the walls with a fury.

But then, as I begin to erase some of the past, the color of the paint, the shade of a spear of lilac burning in the April sun, takes over my thoughts. This expansive field of color, a color just one shade short of hope, leaves no room for the past. The future begins to take over, one that will include a gorgeous room for a nine-year-old girl, one that will be of my own making.

The week I once thought would stretch out like a prison term flies by. The night before they come home, I'm scrambling to hang posters and replace the plain white light switch plates with cheery, colorful ones depicting luminous tropical fish (Jess) and a wise and elegant Siamese cat (Natalie). I line up Jessie's stuffed animals at attention along the back of her bed and arrange the gauzy wildflower curtains in Natalie's room so they frame the view of Mount Rainier. I walk through the rooms over and over, trying to feel the impact of the change through the eyes of a girl of five and then again through the eyes of a girl of nine. For the final touch, I nail the wooden initials *N* and *J* Aunt Kathy gave them for Christmas to their doors.

Natalie bursts through the door first.

"So what's the big surprise, hunh? Don't tell me—you *cleaned*," she says sarcastically.

"Maybe. Wait for Jessica and then I'll tell you."

Jessie comes through the door next, "Okay! What is it?"

"Why don't you two go upstairs?" I say.

Kevin looks at me quizzically, and I feel this flash of irrational fear about having made all these changes without his permission and how uncertain I am about his reaction.

As the girls head up the stairs, I'm right on their heels, not wanting to miss a second. The doors are shut, but the *N* and *J* are visible from the top steps, and when Natalie reaches the summit, she lets out a scream and breaks through the door of her new room like a firefighter arriving on the scene.

"Is it really mine, Mom?" she asks me. It's the first time in a long time that I'm the bearer of anything good.

"Yep! It's all yours, girl. You deserve a beautiful room of your own."

"I can't believe it," she says, stretching out on her new bed under the window.

I cross the hall. Jess sits on her bed, shaking her head. "This can't be true. I've always wanted my own room. Did you know that?"

"You know what, I don't think I did. I knew Natalie wanted her own. But you really wanted your own room too?" I ask, wondering what else she's held in. We're admiring all her stuffed animals when Kevin ducks through the doorway and his hand traces down the wall to the light switch. "You had an electrician come out?" There's some vague insinuation in this question, as if he's confirming that I have, in fact, slept with another man.

I nod, feeling a little guilty although unsure why.

"Who'd you call?"

"I dunno. Rainbow Electric, something like that."

"Hmmm," he says, and it feels like he's trying to decide what all this says about him, and I'm holding my breath, waiting to see what he's going to say, praying that he'll put the girls before his own ego.

"It looks fantastic!" he says at last.

I let out a big sigh of relief and say thanks.

"Tons of work. You must have been working nonstop."

"Pretty much," I say. I look down at Jessie, trying to deflect attention from myself, from the fact that it feels good to be recognized for what I've done.

"I think this is going to work out great," he says. "For all three of you."

"I think so, too," I say, and we both know that the house is no longer *our* house; from this moment on, the house will belong to just the girls and me.

A FEW DAYS LATER, I PHONE MY FRIEND SHEILA AND TELL her about my big week of rearranging the girls' rooms.

"Oh you're in *that* phase," she says.

"What phase? You know about this. You have to tell me. I don't know any other divorced women. All the women around here are sealed drum-tight into their marriages."

"No, no, I've seen this," she says. Sheila's a nurse and for some reason knows a lot of divorced women, even though she herself is married. "All the divorced women I know seem to get really into repainting. This one woman I know, she repainted her living room and dining room one weekend, then repainted them the next weekend. A few weeks later she did them again."

"She kept repainting the same rooms? That seems kind of scary."

"It's a phase. Painting is very metaphoric. New start and all that."

It's weird to think of all this activity as a recognizable phase of human development like the ones children go through—picking up a Cheerio with the pointer finger and the thumb or saying "no" to every request. Apparently I'm not really an individual woman starring in her own never-been-told-before drama. I'm one of thousands, and I'm on a well-trodden path, one with well-mapped crests and valleys and milestones as predictable as the appearance of molars and the onset of puberty.

I fish out *The Divorce Recovery Sourcebook* from underneath my bed, my pulse quickening a little as I read about my past, my present, and my future. The number that gets batted around a lot for divorce recovery is two years, a duration comparable to the average minimum sentence for vehicular homicide. But *Sourcebook* author Dawn Bradley Berry says the period for recovery may be as short as one and a half years and as long as, gulp, four years, depending on the length and intensity of the marriage.

I refuse to accept the four-year number, even though my

marriage was fairly long and I've lost any ability I might once have possessed to judge its intensity. Maybe there's a crash course—sort of a Kaplan type of offering—that could get me out of all this in less than a year? But most of the divorce books say that any attempt to truncate the process—rebound relationships being the shortcut of choice for many looking for a way out of pain and suffering—will merely lull you into thinking you're getting off easy. Usually these diversions, experts suggest, just extend the trip in the long run. I skim through what Berry identifies as the three stages of recovery—reminiscent of Elisabeth Kübler-Ross's stages of grief—and attempt to calculate how much distance I've already traveled.

The first stage is Shock and—what else?—Denial. This stage often begins with a "longer phase" that involves a period of hibernation and time spent wandering in a "personal wilderness." In this stage the person going through divorce can expect to be "stunned, outraged, pain stricken." There is often a depression, a need to reconnect with others for support, and a period of "confusion and wildness," in which the person experiences what sociologists call "anomie," a sense of living outside societal norms, a sort of social vertigo in which the person has no idea of how to behave or what is expected. This anomie and the cutting loose of the bonds of marriage often gives way to "wildness," sometimes manifesting itself in a brief or not-so-brief period of promiscuity.

I've heard about this. Another book I read, *Rebuilding: When Your Relationship Ends* by Bruce Fisher, refers to this as the "horny phase." I read about this in the first debilitating weeks after the split and thought, "Hell no, not me, I'm going to be alone with my kids and not deal with anyone for years and years. Sex just brings trouble."

But lately I've been wondering, "What *about* sex?" Was that it for me, then? Will I never sleep with anyone again? Or might I meet someone—where? The children's section of the library? Can it be possible that sometime in the future I will actually kiss another man and then be heavily making out and then—this part seems foggy—take off all my clothes? It doesn't seem possible that I could still have that in me, that I can go through all those awkward, fumbling steps toward passion with some man who is still unknown to me. But it also doesn't seem possible that I can live out my life without being touched.

Berry calls the second stage Adjustment, a period associated with rage (I've already had a few previews of this), inexplicable guilt (guilt—both explicable and inexplicable—seems a constant throughout this process), and ambivalence about the divorce, sometimes accompanied by a longing to spend time with the ex-spouse. The adjustment stage often ends with—how I loved the sound of this—a "phoenix phase," a time of rising up, letting go, and facing the future with confidence.

The final stage in Berry's schema is Acceptance and Growth, in which there is a releasing of the past. Life slows to a less chaotic pace and there is a feeling of comfort and belonging in one's new life. The person begins to trust again, to take reasonable risks and make solid choices. There is a letting-go of anger and an ability to be friendly with the ex. In all phases of her life, the divorcée has moved ahead.

Reading this, I can see just a glimpse, a little shirttail left untucked, of a time when all this could be true. I don't know how I am going to get there, but I can imagine a future of comfort and belonging. I've felt it before, pulling a blueberry pie out of the oven or watching Jess scooter down a shady sidewalk on a late-summer afternoon or writing in my favorite café. It's a feeling of rightness uninterrupted by pain, a feeling of home. I could imagine its return.

But I also know that this recovery model of divorce is flawed. Some losses—sleep, peace, laughter—are, in fact, temporary; these things will no doubt return to me, boomeranging back through time in that surprising but inevitable way that they do. But there are losses that will not be recouped; some things will be lost forever, just as my twenties and my baby teeth are gone for good. I will never again be the person who married the father of my children. I will never again be a woman married to the only man to whom she ever said "I do." I might recover a great deal of the brightness of my life, but I'm not going to come out of this the same person who went into marriage and then divorce. I'm not sure who she's going to be—this person who's going to rise like a phoenix above all the smoldering embers of her old life. I just want to make sure I'm going to like her.

9

The Good Kind of Alone

One of the few things from the court-ordered custody seminar that stuck in my head was from the list of tips the facilitator read to us: "Take care of yourself. No one else is going to do that for you anymore."

The advice reminds me of a night I was driving down a quiet Utah highway in my 1980 Monte Carlo. I was alone. I was twenty-nine. My life was my own, and I felt the power of that, like I felt the warm, desert night air pouring through the open window. The future receded before me as I headed west toward my little farmhouse and the spot where the sun had set an hour before. Suddenly a spasmodic flash of blue and red lights splintered the night sky as a police officer turned on his siren and indicated that I should pull over. After he told me about my burnt-out left headlight, he turned to go, but then hesitated, crunched back toward me through the shoulder's gravel, and said, "You've gotta get that light fixed right away. If the other one goes, you'll be in the dark out here."

At the time I thought, Hey, no kidding and would you really say such a dumb thing to a male driver? "Excuse me, sir, big driver of black Dodge Ram truck, you do realize if that other light goes out, you'll be driving in the dark, right?"

Looking back, I'm staggered by the profundity of the statement, from the realization that I *am* just one blown filament away from the black of night, that I *am* the only one who could possibly say to myself now, "You're tired. Why don't you go lie in bed with a cup of tea for a while?" or "You're lonely. Why don't you go for a walk with a friend?" I remember that when my dad started in AA, he told me that people in recovery are taught to use the acronym HALT (Hungry? Angry? Lonely? Tired?) as a way of checking in with themselves when they feel like drinking. Again, the simplicity of it seemed shocking (grown people have to ask themselves if they are Hungry? Angry? Lonely? Tired?) and yet amazing. I was intrigued that people met in groups in church basements and admitted to one another that they felt lonely, which seemed a far greater crime to my cool twenty-year-old self than merely drinking yourself near to death.

Loneliness haunted me throughout my twenties. I think the feeling had always been there, locked in some hidden place inside of me—through my California girlfamily days, through my adolescence in my cobbled-together Canadian family. But then, during my first year of college when I was living alone for the first time, some of that loneliness began to surface. It started when my stepsister died of stomach cancer.

Barbara died on Christmas Day. We were visiting some friends of my parents. I never liked the husband, and years later I found out that he had borrowed a lot of money from my mom and my stepfather, Bill, and then refused to acknowledge the debt. He took a phone call in the kitchen, and then came back and said, "That's it. Barbara's gone."

I hated him. I thought he had made this announcement far too matter-of-factly. I was eighteen—I thought I knew how a person would act if he felt sad.

Because my stepfather was Irish, we had a wake a few days later, but it was really an imitation of a wake, because my stepfather was one of the only ones there who was really from Ireland, and he had left at the age of three. So the rest of us just drank too much and pretended to be celebrating the life of a girl of twenty-four who died a few years after earning a bachelor's degree in criminology and before she could ever fall in love. But really we were just sad and Canadian and pretending to be Irish and full of that joyous despair that spawns singers of ballads and a writer who could write about a boy named Michael who died long ago and the snow falling in the darkness of night on Ireland's wild western coast.

And really I wasn't even one drop Irish. I was a step-daughter, a stepsister, an American-Canadian mutt of a girl, an English major at not even a university but a community college, someone constantly a few degrees of separation from the authentic thing—the real grief, the real college experience, the real culture, the real family.

And then suddenly the wake was over. It seemed like it shouldn't end, like we should forever be milling around my (step)aunt's living room of faux colonial furniture and shag carpeting with a half glass of rye in one hand and a salt-and-vinegar potato chip in the other. I was off-center from the real experience—whatever that might be—but at least I wasn't alone.

After the wake, I was dropped off at my basement suite (not a real apartment, mind you, but a makeshift one in an English couple's basement) and I was alone. I wasn't used to drinking hard liquor and I wasn't used to being this alone. My stepsister—the one who'd drunk tea and Benadryl cough syrup with me when we both had colds, the one who might have taught me to drive if she'd liked me more or had been my real sister—was gone, and all those hospital visits—the stilted conversations, the offering of glossy women's magazines, the averted eyes—were behind us. In a week I'd go back to my feverish study of Canadian poets whom few beyond our borders would ever read, but in the meantime there seemed to be no reason to exist, nothing to anchor me to the planet.

And that's when I did the dangerous thing. I turned on the TV.

The show I watched was *Taxi*. Before there was *Friends*, before there was *Cheers*, there was *Taxi* to assure you that no matter how isolated and alienated you felt, there were people out there somewhere hanging out with the quick-witted and the empathetic, feeling connected, and having the *real* experience. The setting of *Taxi* was simple, primarily an unadorned wood table in a cavernous taxi garage, but at that table the drivers (mostly struggling actors) looked one another in the eye, laughed, cried, and by the end of the half hour, baldly admitted their need for one another. The gap between my life at that moment and the camaraderie among Elaine and Tony and Latka was only half the problem. The other source of my alienation was that on what was surely one of the most significant evenings of my life, all I could think to do was watch *Taxi*.

It seems overly dramatic to say that such a small thing as watching a television show can be life-altering, but maybe it's the small things that change who we are. Maybe we can handle the funerals, the stock market crashes, and the landslides that pull our homes down the cliff, but it's those deceptively small things—the act of watching TV alone in a basement suite, the phone call from a friend at just the right moment, the smell of wood burning on a cold night—that transform us at the cellular level. Maybe it's always something small that takes us from hope to despair. Maybe it's something small, too, that takes us all the way back.

It's Friday night, again. Each week I anticipate Fridays with both longing and dread. I long for the evening off from the nightly routine of dinner and baths and home-work. I dread the guilt of finally having what I thought I wanted and the whistling vacancy of a house without children.

Tonight I get a massage I can't afford. I tell the massage therapist everything. I'm putty in her hands. The things I tell her are basically true, yet vaguely inaccurate—the movie version of the real events. This rendition of things sounds af-fected in a way that I find mildly grating, but I've taken on this part and I can't seem to stop myself now. I tell her how sudden the breakup was, how my world split apart over-night. But I also hint that I'm better off than I am—I inti-mate that I can afford this massage, that I do yoga more regularly than I actually do, that I'm the sort of woman whose schedule includes pedicures and Pilates. I tell her about my recent trip to Mexico, but leave out the fact that my mother paid for it. I start to believe in this glamorized image of myself; I picture myself as the sort of divorcée my mother was, the sort that is having a better time than the married women, the sort that wears red Chanel lipstick and high heels with her well-tailored slacks, the sort that knows exactly what to do on Friday nights when her children are with her ex.

The massage therapist tells me things, too. She grew up in a commune. Her father committed suicide. She's in Weight Watchers. We talk about what we eat. We both like apples (2 points) and a certain brand of soft-serve ice cream (3 points). It's like she's my friend except for the fact that I'm paying her and I'm only wearing a towel. I find out she always works on Friday nights, and I feel this enormous sense of relief. I think of Woody Allen saying that he doesn't like to leave New York because he needs to know that if he wants lemon chicken at 3:00 a.m., he can get it, even if he never does. I add her to my Friday-night list. Friday nights have to be managed and planned out. On Thursday I look for movies that begin around twilight or plan to see a friend or to be safely ensconced in an exercise class when the darkness descends. There can be no *Taxi* incidents.

After the massage, I'm walking down the street toward my favorite teriyaki restaurant, feeling all mooshy and mellow, when the cell phone rings. It's Kevin. He's had the kids for three hours. I'm sure he's going to say he's having some work crisis and wants me to take them. I consider not answering. We've been having a lot of bad conversations lately, partly because I've been weaning us off the role I played in our marriage, the one that meant I'd jump in to take over if he was with the kids when an important call came in. And since he's in real estate, there are *always* calls coming in, every one of them urgent. When we were married, my whole nervous system was wired to the phone; no matter what I was doing, one ring of the phone could change everything. By the end of our marriage, I'd begun seriously to question this dynamic between him, me, and the cell phone. Was it normal for one person to have this frantic job without boundaries and for the other to be the little helper person trying to make it all work? Sometimes I'd make pathetic attempts to set some sort of a limit, but this would be met with anger and resistance, and of course, the one thing I couldn't argue with: he was earning our family income.

The phone continues to ring, but I don't answer it.

I walk a little farther down the street, say twenty steps, flashes of fear and confidence alternating within me, and the phone rings again. I look at the incoming number—him again—and my body forgets its dreamy massage and plunges into a vigilant fight-or-flight response. My shoulders are up around my ears. Why does he keep calling? What if something's wrong with one of the girls? But, ah, isn't that how he always gets me? He knows that I couldn't live with myself if one of my kids needed me and I wasn't there. The guilt-ridden, we're such easy marks.

I let it go to voice mail. I decide I will listen to the message and assess the situation.

I listen to the message. A new property was just listed, and his client thinks this is *it*. He wants to see it *right away!* I know the client; he's looked at every house in the city. The man is a Goldilocks who can never find the one that's *ju-u-ust* right. In the background I can hear Natalie and Jess shouting at each other in the backseat. Oh, no. He's driving and agitated and talking on the cell phone while the kids are in the back. I've asked him a million times not to talk on the phone with the kids in the car.

Now there's a war brewing in my head. I want to rescue Natalie and Jessie. I feel as though I've just found out that they're standing outside a burning building. What's worse, after all, than being with a parent who is frantic and desperate to be free of you so that he can go do something else? But I also hear the voice of the therapist, Carla, whom I've been working with since the night Kevin and I split up. She's the one who taught me the voice-mail trick. I'm so codependent I had to be *taught* this. I couldn't think of it and execute it without the counsel of another human being who's positive that all these urgent matters might not be so urgent, and that in fact my sanity and peace of mind might be the most pressing matter of all. And right now she's saying, Don't buy into it. If you believe in all his emergencies, you won't be able to create tranquillity in the children's lives.

I punch in his number.

"I can't take the kids right now," I say, and then add, "I have plans."

"What are they?" he asks, irritated.

I glance into the restaurant to see the familiar orange carp turning like an Olympic swimmer to do another lap in its turquoise tank, the Mediterranean fresco on the wall—a holdover, no doubt, from the last owners. The truth seems so ridiculous. Here he is having a "work emergency," and I can't be with my own children, the children I usually spend my Friday night missing, because it is absolutely imperative that I eat chicken teriyaki alone at a Formica table while glancing aimlessly through the *Seattle Weekly*.

But it's always a work emergency, and it's not often enough that I say no. Carla says it will take a little while to teach him that I am no longer an extension of him, and a while longer for me to believe it. Right now I'm feeling a little like a disobedient arm or foot.

"It doesn't matter what my plans are," I say at last. "I'm happy to help you if you ask me in advance and it works out, but you can't just call and expect me to drop everything."

"You know what you are?" he says. "You're ruthless. All you think about is yourself. You're completely selfish."

"Kevin, the kids can hear you! Please stop," I say, but he keeps going. He says awful things, and then suddenly I realize that I can hang up the phone. If I'm not there, he can't say mean things to me. More important, the kids won't have to hear all this about their mom.

I sit down at one of the window tables. One of the nice Vietnamese owners, the mother, comes over with the plastic menu and the dented metal teapot of jasmine tea. She has a husband and a few grown daughters who work here, too, and one of them is a super-intellectual, hip young woman who studied political science and women's studies at UW. We always used to talk about writers and books when I came in for dinner with the kids and Kevin. She never seemed to mind that Jessie threw her rice all over the floor. Kevin and I would bend over to scoop up as many grains as we could, and she'd always come over and wave her hands and say, "Just go, don't worry about it." And then one day she was gone. I saw her at Christmastime a year or so later. She'd moved to L.A. She was working on a big project to revamp the bus system to make it more viable for the Mexican immigrants who depend on it.

The last time I was here alone—on a Saturday afternoon—the mother nearly broke my heart when she came over with three menus and asked, "Where are *they*? The children?" I felt like I needed to apologize for being alone. Clearly, her children only tore themselves away from her when they were making peace in the Middle East or ending world hunger.

The phone rings again. This time I'm certain I should let it go to voice mail. I order my chicken and pretend to read a movie review. But then I decide I need to listen to the message.

It's horrible. He's telling me how bad I am. He says crazy things about me. Then he says something so ridiculous that it threatens my ability to buy into everything else he's said. He says, "You're not a team player." Incredulous, I play the message again, jumping past the heinous parts, and there it is: "not a team player."

I was married to a person who can actually use the words *team player* without irony, without quotation marks scraped into the air around the phrase. It occurs to me that this in itself might be why we're not together. Carla's suggested to me that the gambling was merely a vehicle for our separation, that because the stakes were so high (two beautiful daughters living with both parents), we needed a big reason to make the split, and gambling was the ticket. Kevin knew I wouldn't leave for less. I was hell-bent on avoiding my family fate, and besides, you can't leave your husband just because he tells you you're not a team player.

Ten years ago I read Alice Munro's short story "The Beggar Maid," about a couple at the ragged end of a long marriage that should never have been for the simple reason that the protagonist, Rose, did not love this man, Patrick, quite enough. They stayed married for ten years, had a child and horrible fights punctuated by moments of ordinary happiness. When I reached the last page, I closed the book and stared up at the ceiling above our bed. The story had lodged in my heart like a bullet. I felt as if Patrick and Rose were real people, friends destined to play out their marriage until its miserable demise. One line, dark and premonitory, etched itself into my mind: "They could not separate until enough damage had been done, until nearly mortal damage had been done to keep them apart."

I go home. Kevin leaves another message: he's leaving the girls with friends for the rest of the evening. I feel like a big bang has detonated inside my family, hurling all its human parts to distant corners of the universe. I have an enormous desire to go grab Natalie and Jess by the napes of their necks and drag them home between my teeth. But then I think of all the ensuing complications—having to explain my erratic behavior to friends, the effect on the kids of being thrust into a situation and pulled from it only moments later. I curl into a little ball on the bed. I'm the worst mother in the world. What would a better mother do?

What would a truly loving, ethical, pure, good person do in this situation?

I call Carla and tell her everything. She can still think clearly. She is at home with her four long-haired cats, her little office attached to her simple house—no ex-husband prowling around the corners of her consciousness. She tells me just what a good person would do and it makes sense and I know I can do it.

I call Jessie, who is at Trish's house, playing with Camille. She doesn't want to come to the phone. Trish holds the phone up to Jessie and she shouts, "I'm having too much fun to talk. 'Bye."

Then I call Natalie at another friend's house.

"Are you okay, Snoopies?" I ask.

"Uh-hunh." She sounds small and far away.

"Daddy was really stressed in the car. Did it scare you when he was yelling on the phone?"

"Is Daddy mad at me?" she asks.

"No, Daddy was frustrated with Mom. He is not mad at you. You haven't done anything wrong. I want you to re-member that. The problems between Mom and Dad have nothing to do with you or anything you've said or done."

"He said you were ruthless."

"I know."

"What is ruthless?" she asks, and even in the craziness of this moment, I still marvel at her innocence, that until today she lived in a time when there was no need to know the word *ruthless*.

"It's a person who doesn't care about other people. But Daddy didn't really mean that. When people are angry, they sometimes say things they don't mean."

"Are you ruthless, Mom?"

"No. I care about you and Jessie a lot."

"Do you care about Daddy?"

"Yes."

"As much as you did when you were married?"

"In a different way, yes."

"Can we go to *Confessions of a Teenage Drama Queen* tomorrow?" she asks, and I know she's okay. At least for now.

STEVE AND PAULA ARE PERHAPS THE HAPPIEST COUPLE IN the world. Steve is happy because after an unhappy first marriage, a brutal divorce, and a long period of looking for love, he met Paula, who is gorgeous, smart, kind, and devoted to him. Paula is happy because, in her mid-thirties, she has finally found a man who makes real sense for her. She is a city girl who grew up trapped in a small-town Mormon life. She got married for the first time at twenty to the cutest boy from her high school and was divorced—despite the laments of her Mormon friends and family—at twenty-five, but all that seems like a long time ago now.

Paula and Steve have this giddy air about them that people on second or third marriages often do. They are utterly delighted to be happily married, both having believed at one time that such a goal was out of reach. Now that they've found each other, they take every chance they get to celebrate their love and each other. Their house is like a little Love Boat floating in the Scottsdale desert of red rock and irrigated lawns the color of emeralds. There are flowers and cards for no reason at all, passionate hello kisses, framed photos everywhere of the two of them in romantic places doing romantic things—in each other's arms on a Maui Beach or hiking in Canada through Whistler's lush summer green.

Paula and I talked on the phone a lot in the first months of my divorce. She was working as a pharmaceutical rep in Phoenix, ferrying samples of arthritis and asthma medications from one doctor's strip-mall office to the next in her air-conditioned company car. We talked about her divorce, how she watched TV in her rented room in the months afterward. Once she was in Target with a cart full of items and was suddenly so struck by how alone in the world she felt that she abandoned the cart and fled from the store.

Paula's been worried about me. When an old friend worries, it's scary. She's charted the distances from high to low in your emotional range; she's seen you bounce back before. When she worries, you can't help but wonder if you'll make it back up to the midline this time. Her coos of sympathy and concern release the feelings I've been holding back, and soon I'm sobbing into the phone and saying, "What am I going to do?"

"You're going to come visit me. That's what. It's seventy-six degrees here, and I have enough frequent-flier miles to buy you a ticket. All you need to do is show up at the airport."

"Really?" I say, sniffing, and I hesitate, thinking about the logistics of child care and what it might be like to stay with the world's happiest couple at this time in my life. "I don't know if I can. I'll try."

"Come here and I'll take care of you," she says—words I find impossible to resist.

It's a warm Saturday morning at the main trailhead heading up Camelback Mountain here in Scottsdale, Arizona. Frantic Spandex-clad hikers in packs of two and four are scrambling past us to—I'm not sure what. Get up and down the mountain before us? Most of them seem pissed off, as though they're heading into morning traffic, not at all as though they're about to ascend what looks to me like one of the wonders of the world. I love this place. I love the saguaros that look like cartoon characters and the dry turquoise air. I love that in the middle of all this crazy gated-community, strip-mall life this ancient sacred place exists, this craggy outcropping of stubborn earth that cannot be cultivated.

We let the angry Phoenicians jostle past us and start up the red-dirt trail.

I've forgotten how fit Steve and Paula are. They're keeping pace with the young frantics, and for a few hundred feet I'm right there with them, small stones spraying out from beneath my tread-bare tennis shoes as I scrabble along the narrow trail. But I seem to be slowing down and they seem to be speeding up and the distance between us increases, at first subtly and then exponentially. They pause for me a few times, leaning on a rock at the trail's edge, but they look so like racehorses detained behind the gate that I wave them on and mouth that I'll see them on their way back. Relieved of guilt, they head out again, and soon they are dots in the distance, Paula's white shirt next to Steve's navy one, moving in perfect unison against the terra-cotta of the hillside. Occasionally, when they reach the top of one of the trail's many ridges, they form a joined silhouette against the morning desert sky.

At last they slip out of view completely, and the tether that joins us is broken. I'm no longer a woman walking with friends. I am a woman alone on the trail. I have a brief urge to lapse into panic and self-pity, but I let it drift by without latching on to it. Couples pass me on the way back to the trailhead, and I notice some are happy and some are decidedly not. Some women laugh into the shoulders of their men, and some women's mouths are drawn into a thin line of grim determination. I note all this with a sort of neutrality of mind. A family passes me—baby noodled into a pack on Father's back, preschooler orbiting Mom in search of snacks and water—and I breathe them in and accept them with the same calmness of spirit. Some people are walking in groups, and some are walking alone. It's a Saturday morning in April in the Arizona desert. To be here is good. To have friends ahead is good. To have two daughters in this world—even in their father's apartment a thousand miles away, watching *ABC Kids Saturday Morning*—is also good.

My stride takes on the rhythm of my breathing. In, in, out, out. In, in, out, out. A stray line from my favorite Talking Heads song snags briefly in my thoughts: "The world was moving and she was right there with it (and she was)." Somehow that reminds me of the hikes I took alone in the Utah desert on Saturday mornings the year before I met Kevin. I would walk up between the red-and-white cliffs of Snow Canyon and my breath would match my feet just as it does now. My thoughts recede further and further from me until the only words left in my mind's outpost rattle quietly against one another like polished stones: blue sky, red rock, breath, breath, step, step, step. I am alone, but I am alone in a magical way. I am afloat on a raft of well-being, moving steadily down an old river with no intentions of its own. I am the real girl having the real experience. Not even one skinny degree of separation between the moment and me. Just the blue sky above me, the red rock beside me, and me awake and safe inside of myself.

10

Reunion

It starts with an e-mail reminding me of the upcoming twenty-fifth-year reunion of my high school graduating class. I'm already planning to go up to Vancouver for that weekend to see Nancy, Sheila, and Jocelyn, my good friends from high school.

I glance through the list of recipients and there's his name, right next to mine, side by side, just as our lockers were in the eighth grade. It was the alphabet that threw us together then, but later, in our twenties, we liked to think of it as destiny. Markos.

I've heard his name from time to time over the years, since we share a circle of friends. They'd told me when his daughter was born and later a few details of his divorce. And even now it isn't a name I can hear without an electric charge running through me. He was the silent boy with the brooding eyes and the foreign name. We were thirteen and fourteen.

I didn't think much about him. He wasn't cool or popular. Also, he hardly ever said anything. He might as well have been invisible.

I was twenty years old and he was twenty-one when he finally got up the nerve to call me. He called on a pretense so ridiculous I barely understood what he was asking. Did I want to go in on sending a telegram to a mutual friend who was getting married in England? I suppose so. Did I want to meet him for coffee? Sure, why not?

It was an early-summer afternoon when we met at one of the most beautiful spots in Vancouver—English Bay, with the dark green majesty of Stanley Park flanking one side, the cafés and Greek restaurants of the West End behind it, and, yawning before us, the blue of Howe Sound, dotted with freighters and the white triangles of sailboats. As we sat on the beach, talking, talking, talking, I wondered whether it was the day I was falling in love with or if it was him. By that night I knew.

We traded our stories that day, or at least the version of our stories we believed to be true at that age. I told him about the broken California girlfamily. He told me how he'd escaped from Hungary at ten. Despite the fact that his father had left the country on a business-trip visa five years earlier and never returned, Markos's mother had managed to secure a visa for a two-week holiday for Markos. With the visa in hand, he'd traveled to Amsterdam and stayed with a Hungarian woman there for a night, then flown on his own to Vancouver to visit his father. When he decided to stay in

Canada, he said good-bye to his mother, his *anyu,* hoping to see her again, not knowing if he ever would.

He couldn't have made up a story I would find more romantic and sympathetic. Images flickered through my mind of his mother, grandparents, and him, huddled in their Budapest apartment, picking up stray broadcasts from Radio Free Europe. I could picture the apartment—the very one in which his grandfather had hidden from the Nazis, the soldiers marching one way through the circular floor plan as the grandfather stealthily walked right behind them. The ceilings were high, the floors polished hardwood. The tall, narrow windows opened onto the courtyard where he had played as a boy.

I asked him whether the police had questioned his family after his father disappeared, pleased that I knew something of the world. I had, after all, studied political science right along with Canadian Lit at the community college. And I'd just come home from backpacking in Europe, which I was positive made me something of a genius on world affairs.

He said they had. He pulled his gaze off the harbor and returned it to me. His eyes, I realized for the first time, were very blue. He laughed a little. "I used to have to pretend to people that he was coming back, but I knew he wasn't."

"That must have been lonely." I looked at him again, waiting for him to admit he'd made all this up. He was leaning back now on one of the many salt-bleached logs washed up along Stanley Park's Third Beach. He was actually very handsome—golden, suntanned skin, sandy brown hair, a kissable mouth. How could someone this good-looking have been so indiscernible to me in high school?

"Hey, how come you never talked to me in high school?" I asked.

"I did, a few times. I dunno. Shy, I guess," he said, drawing a grid in the sand between us with a stray twig.

"If I'd been through all you had, I think I would've told everyone," I said.

"I know you would've," he said with a half smile.

"What does *that* mean?"

"It means you liked to talk *a lot*. You were always talking."

"That's not *true!*" I said, and pushed him on the arm. His shirt felt warm and soft underneath my hand.

He looked at me and smiled. "I must have mixed you up with some other girl. Maybe you were the quiet one." We both laughed, leaning ever so slightly toward each other, still a few hours shy of our first kiss.

I STARE AT HIS E-MAIL ADDRESS ONE MORE TIME AND think about the fact that he can see my name on the list just as I can see his. He's no doubt heard about my split. He'll e-mail me by morning, I think smugly, and go to bed.

A week goes by and another reminder from the reunion committee arrives in my inbox. I realize that he hasn't e-mailed me after all. Humph. Should I e-mail him? He isn't married anymore and neither am I. I could write him and who would care? No one. I sit down at the computer, open the Compose screen, and type in his address. Then I stop.

I know why he hasn't contacted me. Let sleeping dogs lie, he's probably thinking. Why bring up all those feelings from the past again? Why get near all that old hurt? There are certain songs I can't listen to, even these many years later. All the songs we liked back then are fraught with nostalgia and yearning, as if we were preparing ourselves in our year together in our twenties for all the years when we'd be apart. Over the years, I've learned to punch the radio buttons quickly at the first bars of a Springsteen song's aching harmonica or the melancholy strumming of Neil Young, to save myself from longing for a time of unbelievably young hope and joy, a time of driving through the New Mexico desert in a '65 Valiant, sharing a Coke and a cigarette by the side of the road, and talking in bed until the morning light shone through the windows. In our short time together, we'd tapped into two veins of gold that briefly ran together— the freedom of youth and the power of two become one.

The combination was so magical that we assumed we were invincible, like romantic figures from a Dylan song who can outrun the trappings of ordinary life and defy the laws of gravity and the human need for cash. When we were together, we were so happy that we didn't need to bother ourselves with the steps that mere mortals were taking all around us. We could live together before we knew each other, make a living sheerly off fledgling talent, take off for

Australia and make a temporary home in a Queensland rain forest. We would spend our evenings watching the sky fade to dusk, ignoring common sense and listening only to each other, the conversation of tropical birds, and the snapping of twigs under the urgent weight of wallaby legs. So what if we didn't have work visas?

When life caught up with us, we were using the money we'd gotten by cashing in our return tickets to buy potatoes and oatmeal. Markos was climbing on top of the ten-foot-high rain tank to pull our water out by the bucket because we couldn't afford to pay the electric bill that stood between us and an operating pump. I was trying to hawk roadside the second-rate batik shirts I'd made in our kitchen, and he was earning just enough money making pottery to cover the rent for our cottage in the rain forest. And who knew that Queensland had a rainy season? The rain, which was really more like a monsoon, fell in sheets and didn't stop for weeks on end. And who knew that rain would drive all the "fruit rats" (Markos insisted that their diet of mangoes and such made them different from common street rats) into our idyllic bungalow? Who knew that the effects of being broke—even the kind of broke that white middle-class kids bring on themselves—could be felt so quickly? That a girl who loved a boy would turn to sleep on the far edge of the bed, that they would shout at each other about what they were going to do next, that they would look at each other and think the other might be the reason they were in such a mess.

Once we were walking through a botanical garden in Brisbane, Australians in their Sunday clothes ambling among the shrubbery on either side of us, and I turned to him and asked, probably for the thousandth time, "What are we going to do?" He shouted at me, his voice foreign yet familiar, "I don't know! Stop asking me!" So much for birds calling to each other. So much for Bob Dylan. Shame rushed to my cheeks. No one had ever shouted at me in public before. In my family, we shouted only behind closed doors.

I didn't make the connection between the way that Markos spoke to me then and the way his voice dropped a few octaves to a low growl when he spoke to his father in Hungarian. It never occurred to me that being Hungarian was anything more than a good story. It made him interesting to me, but I didn't understand that the culture he was raised in, and that was still a part of him, had affected him in lasting ways. Your father leaving for the other side of the Iron Curtain while you and your mother stayed behind meant something. And being teased for your accent the first time you dared to speak at your new Canadian school could mean years of silence.

But I didn't—couldn't—understand this, so I began to retreat in a quiet Canadian way, and by the time we finally landed at the Los Angeles airport, I'd closed myself off completely. Two weeks later we broke up. I was just a few months shy of twenty-two; *easy* and *fun* topped my list of relationship must-haves. I was sure a relationship shouldn't be this hard, and that my life would be better without him. But even after that breakup, we spent a good part of our twenties coming together and then breaking apart.

I look at his address once again. He has his reasons. If I knew better, I'd have mine. I shut down the computer for the night. I'll leave that bell unrung.

The next morning is the kind of morning in May when anything seems possible. The scarlet azaleas and purple rhododendrons are committing their annual miracle in the front yard. I drink coffee on the porch and feel the sun soak into me. I feel young. I feel like *doing* something, something more than the routine activities requisite for daily survival. It's the same feeling that propelled me through my twenties, but I haven't felt it in so long I hardly know its name. And then it comes to me: I feel *restless*.

I fantasize about running to the beach and back up the long stairway that climbs up a bluff from the blue water of Puget Sound, or maybe flying to New York and walking through the streets until I can't walk anymore. I change into a pair of capris, a T-shirt, and some sandals, and load my laptop into my shoulder bag. I go down to my favorite café, drink an Americano with milk and sugar, and write for an hour, but then I can't sit still any longer. I don't know what to do with myself. There's just three hours before I'm due to volunteer at Jessie's school. What can a person do in three hours?

I go home and check my e-mail again. Nothing. I put on a Mark Knopfler CD loud and go out to the garden. I'll dig and dig until I can't dig anymore. The sound of Knopfler's smoky voice meets me in the garden. I've been listening to his way of seeing the world as long as I can remember, since he sang about the sultans of swing, since he sang about a boy named Romeo and a girl named Juliet. He knows what it means to want, to have a longing you don't know what to do with. I water the peas and tell myself that their progress, their slow ascent up the trellis, is like mine. Sure and steady, as inevitable as the seasons. Then the fifth track starts—a duet with Van Morrison called "The Last Laugh"—and I'm caught completely off guard by the sound of it in the garden on such a warm day in May when the green fuse that drives the flower is breaking ground all around me.

"Don't you love the sound," Van Morrison sings, "of the last laugh going down?" There's only one person who would love that line as much as I do, I think.

I bolt up the kitchen stairs and switch on the computer. I enter his address in the To field. By now I know it by heart. "Have you heard this Marc Knopfler album? It's called *Sailing to Philadelphia*." I write as if it's been seven days since we last spoke and not seven years. "I think you'd like it." I bring the pointer up to Send and click the mouse button. The click sounds like a gun firing at a race.

A few hours later he writes back. He hadn't heard of the CD. He asks how I am. All pretty generic except for one line: "Your '*locker*' is still next to mine."

At seven the babysitter arrives and I go to a lecture with Trish. The speaker has written a novel about the child of

Holocaust survivors. Everything she says is dark and full of portent, and I can barely hear any of it. My thoughts are stirred up by old love and the scent of sweet peas newly in bloom, and I can't quite wrap my mind around human suffering. The only thing I hear her say is, "We meet people and fifteen minutes later we figure we know who they are, but then we can spend a lifetime with a person and realize we still don't completely know them. They can still surprise us."

As we mill out of the auditorium, Trish looks at me, her eyes wide, her expression reverential, and says, "Wow." Trish seems to have read just about every book on the Holocaust. She's not afraid to hold all that awful knowledge within her.

"Yeah, that was something," I say, and then, after letting a respectful second pass, I turn back to our earlier conversation in the car. "So when he said 'your locker is still next to mine,' that was a metaphor, right?"

She looks at me wearily, as friends do when they think you're on the brink of a huge mistake. She lets out a sigh and says, "He's not speaking of actual lockers." And then, indulging me as she would a child, she adds, "The locker represents the heart. What he's saying is, 'Your heart is still next to mine.'"

When I call directory assistance for his number the next day, I half expect the operator to say, "What do you want that number for? You have no business calling people you haven't seen in years and messing with their heads. Why don't you just go take a walk, or, better yet, go do something nice for your children."

Surprisingly, she gives me the number without protest. I dial it and he answers.

"Hi, Markos," I croak. "It's me."

"Hey, you. How are you?"

"I'm good. Or okay, I guess."

"That's good. So why are you calling?" he asks. "Is something wrong?"

Why am I calling? I'm not prepared for this. I'm standing at the kitchen counter with a soapy cloth in my hand. I wipe the counter in long, even strokes.

"I don't know why I'm calling. I mean there's a reason, but I just can't say what it is. Did you hear about me? About Kevin and me?"

"Mm-hm. I heard that." His voice is quiet and gentle. I can't hear even a trace of judgment. I ask who told him and he says it was our friend David.

"Yeah. I heard you were at David's in February. Did he tell you any of the details?" I ask, looking out the window to the backyard, where a squirrel is racing along the sagging roofline of the old garage. I hadn't expected to feel this nervous.

"Nope, just that you guys split up last fall."

"Good," I say a little too abruptly.

"Why?"

"I don't know." I'm struggling for words. It's this odd sensation of talking to someone who seems at once intimate and remote. "I just don't like the idea of someone telling you the whole story about me. You know, like it was just a good story. I remember hearing stuff from your divorce and thought you wouldn't like that."

"Well, that was a long time ago now."

"So I guess you're in a relationship. Maybe you're living with someone?" I wonder if there's some woman in the background—younger, no doubt—brushing her lustrous hair, waiting for him to get off the phone.

"Nope. Just me up here."

I stop wiping for a minute, surprised at how happy I am to hear this. The image of the woman with the lustrous hair has melted away.

"What about you?" he asks.

"Silly! No. I mean I'm not even fully divorced. Legally separated. I can't imagine being involved with someone this quick. People do, though," I say.

"Yep, rebound."

"Yep, not me, though."

"Good."

"Why do you say that?"

"Well, I dunno. It just doesn't seem like a good idea. Not healthy."

"God. I'm so nervous. I'm shaking."

"Why are you nervous? There's no need."

"You always did that. You always tried to talk me out of how I feel. I can't help that I feel nervous. Anyone would feel nervous. I haven't talked to you in a long time. I feel so, so vulnerable."

"*You* feel vulnerable? I feel incredibly vulnerable. I think

I fell in love with you the first time I saw you in the eighth grade and have been in love with you ever since. And you're telling me *you* feel vulnerable?"

"The eighth grade?"

"Mrs. Banks's class. I remember you from the first day," he says very quietly.

"I didn't know that. There's no way I knew that." I'm thinking about that first call twenty-two years ago for coffee at the beach. I had no idea then that he'd been harboring a secret crush, and he never let on in the years that followed. Suddenly it feels as though he was the one common denominator that has run through my fractured life.

"It's true. I always liked you."

"That's very generous of you to tell me that. Very." Words are fighting to come out of me. "I think I know why I called, but I just don't know if I can say it."

"Just tell me," he says softly. "Whatever it is, it's okay."

"It's just that . . . I can't believe I'm saying this, but I also feel like I can't help myself." I sound like a flustered cheerleader. Maybe I should just say "I gotta go," and hang up.

"Whatever it is, it does not matter. It does not matter," he says, and I remember his way of saying a phrase and then repeating it emphatically. I always figured it had something to do with the rhythms of his first language, Hungarian. It reassures me he is, in fact, the same boy I'd known long ago.

I can't hold it in any longer. "I feel like there's something unfinished between us."

There's a silence for a beat, two, three. I have the sensa-

tion of falling, even though I'm still standing at my kitchen
counter, still watching the squirrel worry his way yet again
across the apex of the garage.

And then he says this: "I think so, too."

For the next two days we talk on the phone. Sometimes
the battery on one phone goes dead and I switch to another.
We talk on the phone as I unload the dishwasher, load it
again, take out the trash, and make the bed with one hand
holding the receiver and the other tucking in the corners.
On day three, we decide that I will come up to his place on
an island several hours north of Seattle for a visit. A long,
extended talk. A getting-reacquainted.

I'm excited, but also can't help remembering our last
visit. I was twenty-seven years old and it was the summer of
1989—the tail end of our marathon six-year breakup. At
the time he was living on another little island, also nestled
between Vancouver Island and the mainland. We spent the
day talking, drinking blackberry tea, walking on the uneven
beach with the sound of sea-smoothed pebbles complaining
beneath our feet. We bought a salmon to barbecue.

In a few short hours I was transported back to that en-
chanted realm it seemed we could only access together. The
sky became bluer, tea tasted more like tea, and I felt like I
was *more,* the way I could be under the gaze of someone who
really loved me. Assuming I'd be spending the night, I said
something about the next day's ferry schedule.

And that's when he told me there was another woman in
the picture and that "it wouldn't be fair to her" if I stayed.

Stung with rejection, I left a few hours later, sailing off into the early-summer sky with its streaky clouds of pink and pewter. Somehow the beauty of the evening just made me feel worse. In the past, I'd been the one who'd sent Markos away, and, selfishly, I'd thought he would remain out there, orbiting me faithfully in the distance. But within a year he was married to this new woman, off in another universe. The woman with whom he has a daughter. The woman he has since divorced.

I edit the memory of that visit so that the bluer-than-usual sky is in the foreground, the miserable ferry ride a mere footnote. Two days later he e-mails me a photo of a tiny stucco guest cottage—faded prayer flags strung across one side, a thicket of bamboo shading the other side. He's named the jpeg "yr hut."

Oh, I think. Okay, that clears that up. I hadn't really assumed that we'd be sleeping together, but I hadn't ruled it out, either. Okay. Good. Great. No rushing. Getting to know each other. Sensible. Taking our time. Very grown-up.

I WAKE UP ON SUNDAY, HEAD DRY AND GROGGY FROM talking on the phone until 2:00 a.m. with Markos. Today is Jessie's birthday party at the gymnastics academy. I'm wrestling with RSVPs, a cake, ice cream, a knife, plastic forks, an ice cream scooper, candles, matches ("Important! Don't forget!" I'd written on the birthday to-do list), as well as paper and pen to write down who gives her what so we can generate the requisite thank-you notes. I wonder how we're going to make it out the door with all this. Mama's got a man on her mind and cannot hold a thought for more than one second.

The phone rings. It's a friend of my mom's. My mom's had a small stroke.

"*What?*"

The woman starts talking about types of strokes. She says some acronym—TMJ? No that's something to do with the jaw. Anyway, my mother might have had this "T" type of stroke, and if she did have this "T" type of stroke, that means she'll be fine, just fine, don't worry. We'll know within twenty-four hours. If she stops presenting symptoms within twenty-four hours, she could be okay. Okay, as in just fine. Okay, as in just like she was before. What symptoms? Language loss, mainly. Like saying *telescope* when she's trying to say *elevator*. Jeez.

I e-mail Markos and tell him the news and that he shouldn't count on me coming.

The birthday party is surreal. Six-year-olds in leotards of bubble-gum pink and aubergine, hooting and hollering, leaping ecstatically on the trampoline, diving into pits made of dingy green squares of foam. Kevin and I shift into our public co-parenting roles, the divorced couple so congenial that one seven-year-old actually looks at me with doe eyes and asks, "Theo, why *did* you and Kevin break up?" We shake out the tablecloth and position the Barbie plates with the little pink cups to match. He has agreed to take the kids right after the party so I can go to my mom's an hour away in Olympia. He's being nice, but I feel alone, trapped in a vacuum between the moment when I will see my mom and the riotously happy party children who are leaping and running to the beat of the frantically cheerful "I'm Walking on Sunshine" by Katrina and the Waves. I'm circling the gym, my feet squishing into the sweaty blue vinyl mats, when a text message from Markos arrives on my cell: *En szeterlek.*

I love you.

MY MOM IS LYING ON HER SIDE IN THE FLANNEL NIGHTIE she always wears. She's awake, but just barely. I'm sitting beside her on her bed. It's part of the same Danish teak bedroom set that she and my dad had as young marrieds. It's weird to think that they've been divorced for over forty years and another marriage has come and gone and the set is still in use.

"Mom, I'm going to tell you a secret. Can you keep a secret?"

"Yes, I can keep a secret. I'm very good with secrets." She keeps her head on the pillow as we talk, her eyes sometimes half open and sometimes closed. The linens smell of mothballs and of my childhood.

"You're sure?"

"Who am I going to tell?"

"I dunno. Sisters."

"I'm probably going to forget right after you tell me," she says with a laugh.

"I'm in love. I mean it's kind of crazy. But I know it's true."

"Being in love is the best there is," she says with nostalgia in her voice. "I'm happy for you."

"Thanks, Mom." I'm so touched that she's simply happy for me, that she doesn't say anything like, Oh, is the divorce finalized? Or: Rushing from one disaster to the next, are we? Or: How will this affect the kids? But maybe it's just the stroke that has her forgetting that her daughter is less than a year out of a long marriage.

"And who is this person?" she asks, cheerfully avoiding a pronoun. My mom has become super gay-positive in the last few years. She seems open to anything.

"It's a him. It's Markos," I say, the sound of his name resonating in the air between us.

"Who?"

"Remember from a long time ago? My boyfriend, Markos."

"Yes, yes. He made beautiful . . ." she stops. "I can't think of the word."

This is the first sign I've seen of the stroke, and it scares me to my core. The next twelve hours will be crucial. That's how it is with this type of stroke—a TIA, the doctors call it. If she's still struggling with language recall tomorrow, the damage from the stroke will likely be permanent.

"*Pots* is the word, Mom. He made beautiful pottery."

"Yes, yes, that's the word," she says, and she closes her eyes and goes back to sleep for the night.

I remove the plastic dust cover from my mom's computer—a flashback to the plastic runners that covered our hallway carpets all through my childhood—and start it up. I see that Markos is online and send him an instant message. Markos and his daughter, Anne, use Messenger all the time. I didn't even know what it was until a few days ago. He asks about Jessie's party, my mom.

I type, "I hope I make it up still. It depends on how my mom does."

He types, "We'll see. You're there for her. That's important."

TPN100: But I want to come see you on Thursday.

TEMMOKU: You do what you need to do. We're going to see each other soon. That's the most important thing.

TPN100: I got the photo of the guest hut. It looks nice.

TEMMOKU: Can I tell you something? Totally honestly?

TPN100: *(gulp)* Uh, yeah.

TEMMOKU: I don't want you to think I'm trying to get you up here to get you into bed.

TPN100: Oh. Um, I didn't think that.

TEMMOKU: In the past I might have done that.

TPN100: Oh.

TEMMOKU: What are you thinking?

TPN100: Um, um. I was actually hoping to make it out of the guest hut.

TEMMOKU: Oh, good. I just didn't want to assume.

TPN100: How about if you just assume away? I want to touch you.

TEMMOKU: Mmm. OK, we're thinking the same thing then.

TPN100: I'm thinking it a LOT.

TEMMOKU: Me too.

By the next day, my mom is weak, tired, but otherwise back to "normal." I call the support person at her church and they arrange for bearers of meals and dog walkers to visit her at regular intervals over the next few days. A family friend agrees to spend the night for the next few evenings. I'm free to go home to my kids—and by the end of the week the kids will be heading to their dad's for the weekend and I'll be on my way to Markos.

I wheel my suitcase down the hall. My mom's waiting for me at the front door, clutching her flannel nightie closed at the collar.

"Thanks for coming, dear."

"Of course, Mom. I feel kind of weird about leaving. Are you sure you're going to be okay?"

"Yes. I have my meals, my dog walkers. I'll be fine."

"How many fingers am I holding up?" I ask, holding up a hand.

"Forty-seven."

"Did I tell you a secret last night?"

"Yup. And I don't tell *nuttin* to nobody."

"What was the secret?"

"Can't tell."

"C'mon. I need to know you're okay—you know, cognitively."

"You love someone."

"Who?"

"Markos."

"Okay, good. And get this right and you get a prize: What does he make?"

"Pots. Beautiful pots."

I'M FORTY-TWO AND HE'S FORTY-THREE THE DAY WE COME back together again. It's a cool gray day in late May, the kind we often have here on the western slope of the forty-ninth parallel. Washington State meets British Columbia here in a coastline of granite and Douglas firs with a handful of tiny islands thrown like stepping-stones throughout the bodies of water that divide the Olympic Peninsula and Vancouver Island from the mainland. White ferries motor through the blue of Puget Sound, the Strait of Juan de Fuca, and the Georgia Strait, carrying commuters to work, tourists to holidays, and, sometimes, old friends and lovers to each other.

I walk off the final ferry and it's cold and drizzling.

A tawny beach outlines this side of the island, and just above the waterline a strip of fog hugs the trunks of the rust-colored arbutus trees. We're just across the border, but the light has shifted ever so slightly to a hue that's softer and more northern. The landscape feels more serious, less culti-vated, less forgiving. I recognize it like an old friend in a crowd of strangers, instantly and with all my senses—the jagged tips of the evergreens, the scent of wet earth, the salty taste of the air.

But my main focus is my hair. I have the sort of curly hair that should ideally exist in a desert habitat—a big, arid blow-dryer of a landscape. Microscopic drops of humidity invis-ible to the human eye can cause my hair to triple in size. This morning I spent a great deal of time, energy, and hair product bullying the beast into submission. I pictured myself strolling off this ferry—nervous about what lies ahead, yes, but with good hair and lipstick. I did not, however, factor in the rain, the hair, and the attendant need for an umbrella. Now the moment is here, and I'm obsessing about whether I should collapse the umbrella and allow the drizzle, now rain, to ren-der my hair a snarl of frizz, or attempt to keep it aloft grace-fully while towing my clumsy rolling suitcase at the greatly anticipated moment of our reunion. In which hand should I carry the umbrella? Does the rolling suitcase make me look like an aging Avon saleswoman?

And then I see him. I see his smile first, and then we're hugging and I stand on tiptoes to kiss him and he draws back to look at me and then kisses me and rests his hand on the small of my back and eases me in toward him. The wet black umbrella sits upside down on the dock where I've dropped it.

"I'm here," I say quietly into his neck.

"I kept thinking I was making all this up. But this seems pretty real," he says, laughing. "What's this? A roll-around suitcase?"

"I knew you'd make fun of it. C'mon, let's go."

He grabs my free hand and we head to his truck. We talk all the way home about life on the island, where the library and the lumberyard are. He points out the wooded road where he used to live with his wife and daughter. I'm looking out the window and sneaking glances at him. The last time I saw him he was twenty-eight, intense and slender. Now he's undeniably a grown man with real shoulders, and eyeglasses for distance. On the phone he seemed to be the person I always knew, but now I feel nervous as I sit by this man who—I realize now—I don't *really* know.

We arrive at his cabin, and there's nowhere to sit but the single bed.

"It's like the Bob Marley song—you know, the one about the single bed. Make yourself at home," he says, nodding toward the bed. "I'll go fix us a snack."

I put my suitcase down and walk over to the mirror, adjust my frizzy hair and lipstick. Then I sit down on the bed. I don't quite know how to sit, which position will appear most casual and relaxed. Upright, resting against hands? Too prim. Recumbent on my side, hand propping up head? Too centerfold. I settle finally on cross-legged and leaning against wall.

He comes in carrying guacamole and toasted garlic sourdough, wineglasses, and a split of champagne. "You can take your pants off if you want."

"My pants?" I ask, alarmed.

"They look like they might be tight," he says with a shrug.

"Tight? Like too small for me?"

"Um, no. As in tight travel clothes. I thought you might want to relax a little." He spreads some guacamole on the toast and hands it to me.

"No, I don't. I mean I am relaxed. Thanks. I'll wait. I'll take my pants off later. I mean, oh god, forget it. I'm fine." I bite a big anxious hunk off the toast, the flavors of avocado, lemon, and garlic unfolding in my mouth.

"Are you? You seem, something, nervous maybe?"

"C'mere. I need to talk to you," I say, tugging him toward the bed.

"Can I open this champagne first?"

"Sure." I remember how deliberate in his movements he always was. I was the pup, jumping up, spilling, knocking over cups of coffee, and he was the one sitting down to tie his shoes, bringing the rabbit ear up with precision, double-knotting with determination.

He sits next to me on the bed, opens the champagne, pours, hands me a glass, and we toast to us. He takes a long draw from the glass and says, "Okay, what do you want to talk about?"

"I haven't slept with any man other than my husband since nearly the eighties," I say, looking out the window and then turning back to him, "You know, Duran Duran, MC Hammer, *those* eighties?"

"Okay," he says in his even, calm voice.

"I need you to know I'm scared here. Terrified is more like it." I feel like the saying of all this out loud might have some magical effect. If he knows all this about me, then maybe some of the anxiety will pass.

"Hey," he says, taking my hand. "There's no need. We can just make this whatever we want. Work it out together."

"Come here." I pull his face to mine, turn his head gently, and whisper in his ear, "That was a really nice thing to say."

He turns back toward me and kisses me. My skin tingles as his cheek brushes mine.

We snuggle in together and smile at each other. I remember his smile from so many years ago—the baby tooth that was never replaced by an adult tooth, the way his blue eyes take me in as if I'm all that matters.

"Don't be scared, Sweeties," he says, holding both my hands.

"But this is a dividing line, a point of no return. I cross this and it means I'm really not married."

"You already crossed that line," he says, outlining my hand with his index finger. "You aren't married. If you were, you wouldn't be here." He takes another sip of the champagne and hands me my glass.

It's very good champagne. I glance at the label and imagine him preparing for my arrival, making trips to the liquor and grocery stores. Details and little luxuries were always important to him. When we lived together, he was the one who put the flowers on the table and baked yeasty loaves of bread. For my twenty-first birthday he threw a dinner party and made all the sushi himself.

"But I think a divorce is made up of a lot of little moments. And this is one of them," I say.

He takes my glass and places it on the table beside his. He kisses me hard this time and I kiss him back. I feel the heat of his skin. I bury my face in his neck and breathe in the faint scent of tangerines.

He lowers me onto the bed and we're in this dreamy web of coming together in a rush of kissing and pulling apart to look at each other until a sudden shot of fear breaks through me and I bolt up.

"What is it?"

"Do you realize my kids don't really know where I am? What if there were a real emergency? They think I'm visiting an old friend in Victoria."

"You *are* visiting an old friend, and besides, you have your cell phone. If something's wrong, they'll call," he says, stroking my arm. "I always liked your arms."

"Really?"

"Really." He kisses me, and I'm falling under the spell of the champagne and the kisses and someone who thinks I have nice arms, and we move into this heavenly chain of kissing and a hand straying up and down the back and whispering something sweet in each other's ears. Then he says—his body close to mine, me inhaling deeply the sweet citrus of him, nuzzling his arms—"You know what I'd like to see us do?"

"Mmm?" I murmur into his chest.

"Learn to give each other mind-blowing sex," he says in a matter-of-fact tone.

"*What?*" I scoot as far away as the single bed will allow. "What did you just say?"

"You didn't hear me?"

"Look, you must have me mixed up with someone else. I'm not some porn star. I'm a mom. I bring cupcakes to the school on birthdays and go on field trips. I don't belong here." I fold my knees up and tie my arms around them.

"Oh, c'mon, I didn't mean anything bad. I want us to be special together."

"You didn't listen to me! I told you I was nervous, that I was scared. And what do you do? You put all this pressure on me."

"Hey, it's no pressure, really," he says in a soft voice, half into the pillow, a despondent expression crossing his face like a cloud in front of the sun.

"No pressure. Right! It just needs to be *mind-blowing*. No pressure there!"

"Not right away." He says this slowly, as if this will be the one phrase that will make the whole conversation turn around.

"Great. How long do I have?" I say, and then I feel part of myself close up, that part that isn't ready to trust again. "You know what? I can't do this."

I turn to the wall, wrap myself in what I estimate to be my half of the blanket, and cry. I cry really hard, inhaling in great trembling gasps and wiping my tears dramatically. A good man, I think, would take me in his arms and beg for forgiveness, but not him. He's over there with his back turned to me, locked in silence, just like he always was. Even after all these years apart, I know exactly where he's going—that same faraway cave he's always burrowed into at the first sign of trouble. He could hold out forever there, outlast the best of them, frozen in silence, never coming to coax *me* out of *my* dark space.

He'd always been like this. He was like this in the eighth grade with his brooding eyes and corduroy bell-bottoms. He was like this in the eleventh grade with his puka shells and his scowl. He was like this at twenty and at twenty-five. It had absolutely nothing to do with me. He wasn't *deciding* not to give me what I wanted, what I was sure I needed. When we were younger, these stalemates could extend for hours. But life seems shorter now, and not for the wasting. And maybe this is what love is, after all—knowing who the person is and reaching for them when you know they can't reach for you, going to find them when they are locked up inside themselves, even if you might be hurting or afraid yourself. Maybe this is why we broke up before—because we couldn't talk each other down from our towers. Maybe this is why couples are breaking up everywhere.

Mind-blowing sex. I turn the phrase over in my mind. It seems like something the characters in *Wayne's World* might be after, a cross between a blow job and a really strong bong hit. Maybe lovers carefully trained in tantric skills are capable of mind-blowing sex. But a middle-aged woman fresh from a long marriage, with two young children—is she? What if I *were*?

I trace with my gaze the outline of his head—bare and vulnerable like a baby's, with his hair shorn short along the sides and balding at the top. A vision of his younger self, with long, sandy-colored hair held back by a bandanna headband, comes into focus for a second and then fades back into memory, leaving me alone with the man before me: the sunburned hollow of his neck, the stacked wings of his shoulder blades, the curve of his spine. Physical work has turned him from boy to man, broadened his shoulders and cut elegance into his arms. The person I knew as a boy has evolved, traveled, experienced, and learned. He's built buildings, cut down trees and planted new ones, thrown thousands of pots, helped to raise a child, hoed a few rows, and now he wants to have mind-blowing sex with me.

Then a current of desire jumps through me.

My hand reaches across the gulf between us, the gully where the blanket has collapsed between our bodies, finds his face in the fading light. My mouth moves quickly toward his, and I kiss him. He kisses me back like he knows the distance I've just traveled to find him. Our bodies, rigid just a moment before, right themselves quickly so that we are face to face, eye to eye. We look at each other dead-on. And then we kiss the urgent, crazy kisses of a couple in a war zone with bombs dropping all around them, the kisses of teenagers in the backseat on a warm and starry night, the kisses of a man and a woman come back together at last.

A day and a half later, I travel back along the same path—a truck, a boat, a bus, a boat, a car. I travel with the foggy cheer of someone newly in love and with the innocence of someone who has no notion of how tedious this trip would be as a regular commute. I replay scenes of bliss in my mind—bodies moving slowly and then swiftly under sheets, bodies finally intersecting. Our parting was tender but wrenching. When will we see each other again? How will this possibly work? What will I tell the kids?

Part Three

Acceptance

Go to the edge of the cliff and jump off.
Build your wings on the way down.

—RAY BRADBURY

11

Love in the Time of
the Parenting Plan

Before my marriage ended, I saw divorced moms as untouchables, a class of people whose lives had cast them into a dark and lonely sea, tossed about by the waves and dragged in and out with the tides, perpetually removed from the brightly lit shores of happiness. I remember feeling unabashed pity for a divorcing mom I met when Natalie was in first grade. From my secure perch, I looked on at what I perceived to be the misery of her dreary new life and thought, That's it for her. But lately I've been noticing that the divorced moms aren't necessarily more miserable than the married ones. In fact, many of them seem to be unapologetically happy.

I spot a fellow divorced mother, Kari, at Jessie's school. She's wearing cute low-rise jeans and a ball cap and laughs mischievously into her cell phone while the other mothers straighten backpacks and chat with one another. She doesn't have the trademark beleaguered and frazzled look most of us sport as we shepherd our kids through our morning routine in our gray sweatshirts with a couple of coffee stains dribbling down the front. Kari wears clothes from the juniors' department and has the smug air of the WFW, the well-fucked woman. She and I start talking in the parking lot and quickly exchange divorce stories. She's a year and a half further into the process.

"You seem like you're doing okay," I venture, hoping to find out a little of her secret.

"Well," she laughs, "I have a boyfriend. That helps!"

"You do?" I'm a little surprised how open she is. No tone of guilt here.

"Oh god, yes! And he is fabu*lous*." She pronounces this last syllable with the breathy emphasis of a drag queen.

I drop my gaze to the pavement and whisper, "So do I."

"Co-ol!" She calls out, nodding and giving me the you-go-girl look.

A few weeks later at basketball practice, one of the married mothers is idly cleaning out her purse as a cluster of us sit hunched on the bleachers, only half watching our kids' attempts to dribble balls down the court. Sighing, she passes me a Victoria's Secret coupon from her discard pile. "Do you want this?" she asks, with a tone of despair. "I'm afraid you're the only one of us having the kind of sex that requires good underwear."

I take the coupon from her somewhat guiltily, as though

the whole world will now know that I've broken the one-year rule.

The notion that you have to wait at least a year after a divorce before introducing your child to a new significant other is so pervasive in our culture that I can't say when or where I heard it first any more than I could tell you where I first learned about the mechanics of JFK's assassination or the Golden Rule. It's public domain. You just know.

While undoubtedly humane and well founded, the waiting notion is predicated on the assumption that the newly single parent will be dating eligible candidates living within a thirty-mile radius of her home, in a dispassionate, even clinical manner—meeting discreetly on her evening off for a sequestered dinner, a movie, maybe even a round of Scrabble and a quickie at *his* place. In my image of this type of dating, the newly single parent is no more attached to these various candidates than she might be to blouses on the rack at Macy's. She's merely trying them on. Nothing she can't live without.

Even my friend Nancy (also split from her husband, but normally far too sensible to become hypnotized by the competing voices of advice books) cites the one-year rule to me as if it's recorded in stone and kept in the Ark of the Covenant.

"Aren't you supposed to wait a year?" is her only response after I tell her about Markos coming down to my house for the weekend, even though I'm careful to add that he slept on the couch and that I introduced him as just an old high school friend.

"Yeah, you are," I say in an irritated voice. "But sometimes your life just happens and then you have to work with that." For Nancy, the electrician, the world works as a binary system; something is either on or off, *a* or *b,* yes or no. For me, there will always be a thousand steps between on and off: almost on, flickering, close to off, dimming, ostensibly off.

"All the books say a year," she returns.

"Okay, but couldn't there be an exception?" I plead, unsure who I'm more anxious to convince—Nancy or myself.

And what if the newly single parent falls dizzily in love with someone who lives too far away to be kept partitioned off from the rest of her life, whisked in and out between Friday at three and Saturday noon, when she turns into a pumpkin once again? What sayeth the rules then?

But like I said, it isn't just Nancy. For a divorced mother of two, sensible people seem to agree, falling in love should have a waiting period, like the purchase of a handgun. And in my heart I agree with them. Obviously it's not a good idea for the kids to be exposed to a constantly changing cast of characters, to be told this guy's important this month and then this other guy's the one the next.

But I just want them to know *one* guy. Maybe, though, it's one too many. They're still tender from all the changes that have already happened. They want every aspect of our lives, particularly *my* life, to stay the same as it was before the split. They want—and I'd like this, too—for me to remain in my role of stay-at-home mom, even though I am no longer married and no longer have either the emotional or financial support needed to maintain that role. They see my life as something like the bedroom of a child gone off to college. Secured museum-tight, the room holds time still, a tribute to an era forever past that no one quite has the heart to disassemble.

As a parent, I've always felt that the rules—whether it's no more than an hour of TV a day or no dating for the first year—are all I have. My early parenting looked a little like my first days of teaching, when I read off little note cards instead of free-falling and trusting that the knowledge was there within me. After all, I'm from the tribe of women who didn't really like children, who eschewed domestic life for something more intriguing. When I had children, I was fully prepared to overcompensate for my failings, but I wasn't sure how. With very little tangible knowledge handed down, I had to rely on my own instincts, in which I had so little faith that I spent a great deal of Natalie's early childhood figuring out how all the other moms were parenting and then stiffly mimicking them, like an awkward Jane Goodall trying to break her way into chimp society.

I memorized *What to Expect the First Year* and went on to devour *What to Expect the Toddler Years*. I was neurotically and tediously obsessed with my own perceived shortcomings as a mother. I cubed chicken into minuscule niblets; I checked, rechecked, and checked again the instructions on the use of the car seat. At the same time, I felt that all my efforts were undone by my tremendous yearning for something more compelling to do than stuffing Play-Doh back into its containers, a longing that fostered a free-floating anxiety that sent me running back to the Children's Tylenol bottle to see if it had, in fact, said two teaspoons and not one.

But the fact that Mommy spent part of their childhood wishing for more seems the least of my kids' problems now. I'm so far from delivering to my children the by-the-books childhood I was once sure would save them from their distracted mother that I can only grope through each day, straining to catch that faint voice I can barely still hear—my own. I'm in a sort of recovery from years of being hooked on advice and tenaciously clinging to the "right" thing to do. I've stopped tracing the steps of other mothers because most of the ones I know are married and my trail has diverged so far from theirs that they are of little help to me now. I do know I'm not going to be coming up with the theme for this year's school auction or heading up the PTA. And I know that to bring us through this divorce, I have to keep my goals incredibly simple or I'll start confusing what I need to do with what I think I ought to do.

I make a short list in my head. I will keep them safe from harm. When they speak, I will try to listen. No, I *will* listen. If they speak of feelings that are honest and scare me because they illustrate beautifully how greatly I've failed them, I will try to stay with the fear and not stuff frosted cupcakes in their mouths to stop them from speaking. I will be honest when required, but will leave the business of grown-ups to the grown-ups. I will stop ending everything I say to them with *okay?* as in, "If you yell like that again, you won't be going to the video store later, okay?" I will tell them that no matter what, they will always have two parents who love them.

But I can't expect to save them from hurt or from the fact that their parents are divorcing. I can't always make them happy. It *is* tense on Saturday mornings during the hand-offs. There *will* only be one parent on the blanket at the end-of-the-year picnic. Christmas will probably always be a series of tricky compromises—two trees, presents shuttled between houses. And Mom will sometimes be slow-dancing in the living room with a man who is not their father. But maybe all this could be true and I could still be an okay mom, or even a good mom. And maybe, just maybe, because all these things are true and I am no longer going to pretend that they aren't, I can finally be both a mother and myself.

Still, I don't plan to go completely on instinct, so I go to the library and search the online catalog for books on parenting after divorce, which brings up truckloads of hits. I take a few out, skim the ones with the most rudimentary advice, and toss them aside. Then I start on *Helping Children Cope with Divorce,* a book so smart about children and the cycles of divorce that I find my hands clenching the pages as I read. It's as if suddenly I can see myself not just as me going through my own struggle, but also as "a parent going through a divorce."

It surprises me to see the far-reaching effects of a divorced parent's guilt on the *child*. I have been thinking of the cloud of guilt that envelops me as my own little problem.

But now I learn that the parent's guilt often causes her to pull into a tight little ball of depression right when the children need her to be up and out of the bed and dealing with *their* feelings. I remember how many times the girls had to repeat what they'd just said because I was too lost in my own melancholy to hear them. Also, the book stresses how guilt undermines the parent's ability to say no and discipline effectively, so that the parent can end up "plead[ing] with the child to behave." Ouch. I've definitely done some pleading, as in "Please, please, please, please, *please,* listen to me!"

The other issue that *Helping Children Cope with Divorce* makes clear for me is how tenacious certain thoughts are in the child of divorce. It seems impossible to me that my children could think they are to blame for our divorce, but the book is so emphatic that they will, and that they will need great reassurance from me to dispel this belief, that I approach both of them, and sure enough, hidden under their shells lies the fear that somehow they carry some blame for what has happened. The "reunification fantasy" is another thought that dies hard. Even when a great deal of time has passed or the parents are involved with new partners, children often dream of a time when their mom and dad will get back together once again, sometimes as a way to avoid their own painful feelings about the divorce.

But it isn't just my parenting I'm learning about. As I read farther into the book, my own experience as a child of divorce—a part of myself I'd almost forgotten—snaps into focus. I stumble across a section about how after a divorce the parent and the child can subtly switch roles in a process called "parentification," and I get the odd sensation of having myself reflected back to me, as though I am looking in a mirror.

For days on end, I can't stop thinking about this parentification concept. I call Trish, eager for her take on this. We've talked a lot about how growing up as children of divorce sculpted who we are, how we can't ever seem to stop waiting for the floor to drop out from under us. Trish and I share a family history marked by strangeness. Her father kidnapped her brothers and her sister. He tried to take her as well, but Trish stood up to him and refused to get in his car.

"You've got to hear this," I say, "I can't believe how much sense this makes."

"Okay," she says, "I'm ready for something that makes sense. Go."

I read her the description of parentification, then skip to the part I know she'll appreciate: " 'These children, who may try to solve the problems their parents are having with loneliness, alcoholism, depression, or society, take care of their parent at the expense of their own needs.' "

"Woof," she says.

"Woof what?"

"Woof that was me. Exactly me."

"Okay, I thought so. Me too, but get this part, this is so me it's scary: 'These children, who are turned into pseudo-adults and confidants, are often described as perfect or wonderful, but they suffer adverse consequences in the long run.' "

"Perfect—that was me. My brothers and my sister used

to say, 'Trisha's the perfect one.' It took me years to realize how much that bothered me."

"And I was 'wonderful,' " I tell her. "People used to say what an angel I was. I don't want to do this to my kids. What if I do? What if I'm doing it already and I don't even know it?"

"You're not and you're not going to. If you start to do it, I'll tell you, okay?"

"That sounds like it would work," I say. "I just don't want to be one of those Greek tragedy people who do everything to avoid their fate and then go slamming headlong into it anyway."

"Hey, the kids are arguing about something now. I gotta go. Don't slam headlong into anything."

I hang up and an image of myself as a child comes to me. I was home alone, sitting at my mother's long teak desk, a black rotary telephone on one side and a big blotter pad in the center. I was looking at the nibbed pen my mother dipped in green ink to write payroll checks, when the phone rang. It was a man, a friend of my mother's. He wanted directions to our house from the Bayshore freeway. That was easy. I issued him turn-by-turn directions that would take him right to our house. At the end, he asked how old I was, and I told him I was seven. "That's impossible!" he said. "I've never heard a kid talk on the phone like that. You must be a huge help to your mom. Keep it up!"

One of the unspoken requirements of life with my single mother was that I be the "good one." My mom had a business, a married lover, and three daughters, one of them living in Mexico. She had a lot on her mind. So it was up to me to be good, to know everything I needed to know, to be on the constant lookout for myself—know what papers to bring to school when, where to keep the money from my Girl Scout cookie sales, how to heat up a can of cream of mushroom soup for myself. I watched a lot of Shirley Temple movies on the black-and-white TV when I was home alone, and I hoped people might be reminded of her when they saw how neatly I dressed and how helpful and kind I was.

But then all of a sudden one morning, I froze up. I was eight years old and my mom, as usual, had left for work before I'd woken up. Most days I went through my morning routine on my own, got myself out the door, lunch bag in hand, and walked the five blocks to Loyola Elementary. But on this morning I stood in the middle of my room. Frozen. I had no idea what to do first. I thought of all the things I had to do in the morning: brush teeth, brush hair, dress, eat breakfast, wash face. Images of a toothbrush, a hairbrush, a bowl of cereal started to circle around me as stars do around the heads of knocked-out cartoon characters. I couldn't remember which of these tasks should come first, and it seemed catastrophe would strike if I performed them out of order. The house suddenly seemed like an enormous empty cave, and I was terrified of what might be in the next room. The world felt hollow and devoid of any human voice. I started to cry.

I made it to the phone and called my mom at work.

I told her I didn't know what to do and she told me to get a piece of paper and make a list. So that's what I did: I wrote "eat breakfast, brush teeth, brush hair, get dressed . . ." and then worked my way through the list and stumbled out the door. But by the time I had left the house I was a different person. I was a young girl who knew what it felt like to get lost in her own home.

WE'RE AT THE BALLARD LOCKS, A GIANT SYSTEM OF PUSH and pull that allows the fresh water from Lake Washington to meet the cold seawater of the Puget Sound. It's the first real outing for the four of us—Markos, the girls, and me. We pick our way slowly through the maze of walkways that allow only one person at a time to pass through. No alliances can be formed or broken, so we just walk—Natalie in front, Jess next, then me, and Markos taking up the rear. Sometimes we line up like birds on a wire and lean over the white metal rail to watch salmon leaping like boomerangs through the air, hell-bent on getting back upstream. Then Natalie bolts forward again, and the rest of us march in line behind her.

We arrive home as the sun tips behind the Olympic Mountains and the softness settles in. It's one of those magical evenings of early summer in Seattle, when each day floods with light until well after ten, and then at last a soft twilight hushes the brassy riot of the day. Sprinklers rotate over lawns. Voices, the odd burst of laughter, and the reassuring scrape of cutlery against plates float out of open windows where lights are coming on one by one. We're still not used to being together as a group. We're each—in his or her own way—struggling to make it work, to accept a transplant into the body.

I make Caesar salad and pasta while Natalie interrogates Markos in the dining room and Jess does her best to be noisy and distracting in a giant effort to divert Markos's attention from her sister.

"So how old is Anne?" Natalie begins.

"Eleven. No. Eleven and a half."

"Where does she live?"

"With her mom, on the same island I live on."

"So you were my mom's boyfriend before you were married to Anne's mom, is that right?" she asks, sounding not unlike a prosecuting attorney. I know where this is heading, but I don't want to interfere with their fragile attempts to get to know each other, so I stay quiet in the kitchen as Markos heads into the lion's den.

"Quite a while before, yes," Markos says, his voice growing small.

"Did you think about my mom when you were with Anne's mom?"

"Well, of course, I thought of her from time to time," he says without inflection and then quickly comes in with, "Did I tell you that Anne was in *The Jungle Book*?"

"The movie?" she asks.

"No, they did a play of it. This spring. It was amazing."

"Who was Anne?"

"Mowgli."

"But Mowgli's a boy," she says, stepping in a little closer.

"A girl can play a boy."

"In Shakespeare's time, boys played all the parts," Natalie says, showing off what she's learned in school.

"That's right," he says.

"What about the fire?" Jess pipes in. "How did they make that?"

"I was wondering about that myself," Markos says. "That actually worked really well. What they did was they took a big Indian brass pot and stuck a flashlight on the bottom. On top there was red plastic cut into the shape of flames that the light shined on. It looked very real."

I glance over and see that he has both children's interest, a formidable achievement. I feel a little thrill over how well the evening is going, and then hold myself in check. It's too soon to say. I have to let things run their course. I set the table around them as Markos gives an account of the play and Anne's performance. It's odd to be setting the table for four again. Once in a while Anika comes over for dinner, but mostly we've been three at this table for a good while. When Kevin was here, he sat at one end of the table, I sat at the other, and the girls sat along the side that faced out the window. After the girls knew their dad wasn't coming home, Natalie slid into her dad's position at the head, leaving Jess between us in the lone "child's place." No one will usurp Natalie's position tonight. Markos will sit beside Jessie, with the window view of the tallest laurel hedge known to man.

After dinner, it's bedtime, and, like a high school girl itching to get out of the house to meet her boyfriend, I'm anxious for the moment when I can be alone with Markos. After a little resistance, Jess is willing to go off to bed, bribed with a promise of a bedtime story told by Markos. Natalie, on the other hand, wants to remain wedged in between us, as the keystone that holds the bridge of her family aloft. Finally, I insist that she brush her teeth and she clomps off to the bathroom. After a few minutes, I realize she's still in there. I go to the door and knock. She's lying on the bathroom floor, something she's never done before.

"I don't know why, but I just feel so bad. I feel horrible."

"I know you do, sweetie," I say, and I stroke her hair.

"I don't want him here."

"Okay."

"What does 'okay' mean?"

"It means I hear you. I know you don't want this. I do know that."

She cries against me for a little while and finally she lets me tuck her into bed. I try to leave after ten minutes, fifteen, and twenty, and each time she stops me, tells me she can't sleep, that she needs me. I stay, telling myself that soon she'll drift off. I feel myself bifurcate down my centerline like those tadpoles in tenth-grade biology. I sense the presence of two distinct selves: one desperate to comfort my daughter, the other selfish, greedy, eager to dive into the big chocolate cake of new love.

The first few times that Markos comes to visit when the

kids are home are sometimes quite blissful in a faux-family sort of way, and other times akin to a root canal. He sleeps on the couch because it seems too early for him to be sleeping in the same bed Mom and Dad slept in together less than a year earlier. I wake up at five in the morning and creep into the living room and lie beside him, wishing I could freeze time and stay tucked in his arms all day, but at the first footfalls upstairs, I leap off the couch as if I've just received an electric shock, just as I did when I was sixteen and heard my mother start down the basement stairs to check on my boyfriend and me.

One rainy afternoon, I go to lie down in the bedroom, wanting a break from the four of us. Markos comes in and lies down beside me, and I go to touch him—wanting just to kiss him—but then Natalie plunks into my desk chair and spins, browsing with obvious glee through my normally forbidden papers until I shout, "Hey, that's enough!" and find myself awash in remorse and guilt.

It is excruciating to watch Natalie struggle with how to just *be* when she is around Markos. She cycles through a gamut of emotions, from disdain to giddiness, in five-minute intervals. Sometimes she'll be very nice to him, but then glare at me or make a snide remark when he leaves the room. He'll somehow return just as I'm telling her to smarten up, and he'll look at me surprised and come over and rub my shoulders and say something like, "Hey, easy there." And then she'll say something like, "Yeah, Mom," even daring once to add, "Why don't you chill?"

. . .

A FEW DAYS AFTER MARKOS LEAVES, WE'RE BEADING
necklaces at the dining room table. I don't often bead necklaces, or do any sort of craft project for that matter, so I'm
feeling a little like the archetypal super-involved, hands-on
mom. Natalie looks up and in a suspicious tone—a tone
not unlike the one Rita Moreno uses on Natalie Wood when
she realizes Wood has fallen for a member of the rival Jets
gang in *West Side Story*—she asks me, "So, are you 'in love'
with him?"

She is the girl and I am the grown woman, but still I
tremble a little as I nod my head.

She looks at me with the exasperation of a mother of a
teenage girl and says, "So soon?"

"It's not like I *planned* for this to happen now. If I
could've chosen a time, I would've waited."

Jessie nods and tries to make sense of it all by drawing
from her far-too-extensive knowledge of Disney films.
"Yeah, in the movies," she says, "when the characters fall in
love, it just happens. They don't *know* it's going to happen."

Natalie turns her frustration on Jess. "Jessica, can't you
see this? Mom and Dad are a match. For every person there
is just *one* person. Dad is that person for Mom. There cannot
be another person!"

Resting her head on one hand, Jess looks strangely detached and beatific, a little like the Dalai Lama, as she says to
Natalie very calmly, "I don't believe that. I think there can be
more than one. Wait here. I'll show you."

Jess leans over the front porch and plucks two waxy camellia leaves from the overgrown bush that borders the house. Carefully she tears the first in half, but before she does this she waves the one whole leaf that symbolized her parents' intact marriage before our eyes, like a magician gesturing to show that he has nothing up his sleeve. Then she calmly demonstrates the autonomy of the two newly freed halves and the ease with which the mother half of the first leaf is able to hook up with the male half of the second torn leaf.

"See how the leaf can split in two. I think," she pauses and then continues in a measured, emphatic voice, "there can be more than one true love."

I sit there speechless for a moment, and then Natalie spins on her heel and dashes to the same camellia bush to yank off another leaf.

"Well, this is what I think," she says, looking me right in the eye as she waves her leaf in my face. "This was Mom and Dad." She then shreds the leaf violently into minuscule pieces, shouting, "This is them now."

I am terrified of her anger and the enormity of the situation. I know her anger is justified, and I know, too, that I'm the one who has set the match to this blaze of emotion. But, scary as that is to realize, I am also relieved. Maybe now we can start to move forward. I pull her close to me and hold her for a long time while she cries and cries, and I say the words I can only hope are true: "It's okay, it's okay, it really is okay."

12

This Too Shall Pass
(But No Time Soon)

Jessie's guitar teacher, Jane, is a funky cool rocker mom whose son is in Jessie's first grade class. She has a few bumper stickers on her VW van that I noticed even before I spotted her in the school halls with her leather jacket and big smile. One says GOD, PROTECT ME FROM YOUR FOLLOWERS; another says REPUBLICANS FOR VOLDEMORT. Her guitar case sports a Violent Femmes sticker and a Bodeans one. She talks in a fabulous Arkansas drawl about whatever is on her mind: how archaic the divorce laws are in Arkansas, where her ex still lives, the music business, or—when Jessie is out of earshot—about how much she likes beer and sex. I like her because she's not like other moms, and she really *gets* Jessie. She said to Jess one day, "I saw you in the hall at school and I said to myself, 'That girl there she is special, she reminds me of me when I was a girl. She's a *muuuusician.*'" Jessie liked that, a lot, and so did I. When she heard that

Jessie was doing martial arts, she said, "Jess, yoga opens up the soul, but martial arts, that's how you guard it."

One day, after Jessie's lesson, Jane tells me in her Bill Clinton voice about her mom. "So," she says, "after forty years of marriage she gets this idea she's gonna divorce my dad and go live by herself in a condo down in Florida. And I say, 'Okay, Mom, if that's what you wanna do.' And she says to me, 'In three weeks, I'll be a free woman.' And I say, 'Oh yeah, is that what you think?' And my mom says, 'Yeah, that's what the lawyer woman told me.'"

Jane looks at me like we're both in the same club, which we are, and that makes me feel quite a bit cooler than I really am, and she says, "'The *paperwork,* Mom, the paperwork might take three weeks. That's not the divorce. The divorce takes years and years. You might die before you're really done with Dad.'"

THE ISLAMIC TERM FOR A "REPUDIATION OF MARRIAGE"— known as the "triple talaq"—allows a man to divorce his wife by saying to her: *talaq, talaq, talaq* ("I divorce thee" three times). The simplicity of this is breathtaking. My divorce process, while not nearly as complicated as some, has been quite a bit more drawn out than the triple talaq.

But today I said my final good-bye, standing beside my boyfriend in a courtroom stuffed on one side with people stricken with fear and misery and on the other with indifferent civil servants watching the clock stroke its way toward lunch. My attorney has sent a paralegal I've never met in his place. Is this normal? Should I worry? Complain? Do I get a discount on his $225-an-hour rate, even though he has texted her to tell me that he's sorry?

She's well coiffed, overweight, and perspiring in her Ross Dress for Less winter suit. She's extremely nervous—more than I am, which doesn't seem quite right. I make a few comforting noises and tell her it's okay. It's hot in here despite all the fans whirring, fluttering all the highly important papers, and every few minutes she dabs her brow with her handkerchief. I find myself obsessing about her handkerchief. My stepdad always carried a handkerchief. His were sent every Christmas from nearly forgotten relatives near Belfast. How many people still carry handkerchiefs? They seem so melodramatic and antiquated, like the word *swoon*. Where do you even buy one? She must have anticipated the need for a hankie this morning, must have foreseen forehead-dabbing and packed it in her purse along with her lipstick and cell phone. It's going to be a hot one—better bring the hankie.

I've only been to this place twice, the last time some ten months ago with my husband, the horrible afternoon of our legal separation. But he's not here today. My attorney said he didn't have to be, and he'd better be right. I don't want to go through all this just to have the judge say, "What do you mean, he's not here?"

Eventually the judge summons me. She doesn't quite fit my image of a judge; she's about fifty-five, with a bubble hairdo and a silky purple sleeveless shirt. I'd like a tad more formality for this defining moment—a British man in a black robe and a powdery wig, perhaps. She asks me three times if I am the person named on the document in front of her, stumbling—as people often do—on my first name, Theo, which seems like it ought to belong to a man.

"That *is* me," I say. I feel anxious to get this over with before someone blows a whistle and announces that some needed piece of paper is missing and ends the whole charade.

"Okay," she says, visibly annoyed, "sign here and here and here and there."

I sign nervously four times and push it along the blond oak desk back to her.

She stamps it once, hands it to the sweaty paralegal (dab, dab), and says to her, "She's done." The paralegal has her trapped-fawn look working, but manages to grasp the paper and turn toward the anteroom.

"Excuse me," I say to the judge. "What did you mean by 'she's done'?"

She looks me straight in the eye, her voice rising with impatience. "You're done. You can go," and swivels toward the next attorney and client in line.

"But when you say 'done,' you mean divorced, right?"

She swivels sharply and looks at me, incredulous. "Yes, that's right."

"Okay," I say to Markos, "let's go." We leave the paralegal in a hopelessly long line to record my divorce with the county and jet out of the anteroom. We can't stand to wait for the crowded elevator, so we take the stairs even though we're on the fifth floor and the stairwell smells faintly of urine. We descend the cool, dark stairs down and down, all the way to the ground. Then, pushing the bar on the door together, we burst back into the light.

Outside, the city is oblivious that my life has been irrevocably altered. The sidewalk is full of lawyers in summer suits balancing coffee cups, briefcases, and cell phones and ordinary people in khaki shorts and T-shirts or the stiff clothes they think will help them fare better in court. There's some construction near the courthouse, so scaffolding and boarded-up sidewalks and guys in hard hats are part of the mix.

"What do you want to do now?" Markos asks.

"I dunno. Get the hell out of here. How about jump on the next bus, go home and take a nap?" I say, my head swimming with finality and street chaos.

"But we're downtown already. We should do something good."

"I'm not hungry. I know that."

"Hey," he says, lighting up, "let's go see the new library."

This is the last thing I want to do. I don't want to mince quietly around new architecture, oohing and ahhing at the details. But he seems to really want to go. He'll probably love reading the little brochures about how the design came to be, why the ceilings are vaulted just so, the advantages of the floor plan. And what else are you supposed to do after your divorce has been finalized? High tea? Impulse shopping? Shots of single-malt scotch?

I tell him I'll go.

"It'll be fun," he says, giving me a squeeze.

We walk toward the library in silence, hand in hand, breaking apart once in a while to let a passerby through. There's a comfort in this silence. My old friend is with me on this day, my old friend who loves me. But still I am sad. This has been a crazy summer of mixed feelings—the melancholy of divorce, the thrill of new love, the exhaustion of parenting alone, and the random sparklers of joy about a new life of my own, crackling brightly against the night sky. It seems like *this* is what divorce is—after the misery, it's mixed feelings that just won't quit.

ONE OF THE BIGGEST MISTAKES I'VE MADE HAS BEEN seeing our split as the end of our relationship. Somehow I hoped it would just be *over,* like breaking up with a college boyfriend. It isn't. We aren't married any longer, but because we both love and take care of our daughters, we are still in a relationship, with decisions to be made and issues to be discussed. But emotionally we have no real desire to progress, or means to do so, so our dynamic remains frozen at the low point of the day we broke up—or, more accurately, we're suspended at the less operatic, more ordinary low point we were at the day *before* the chicken and the drama, the day I think of as the last real day of our marriage.

We hadn't been getting along well, but not in a way that I would've considered grounds for divorce. We had two daughters we adored and brought into the world together, and yes, we'd had a lot of arguments in the last year, and yes, they seemed, to me, increasingly unsolvable, and yes, we'd already done couples therapy so we knew how to state our feelings so that the other person could hear us and how to listen so they felt heard. We knew all that good stuff, but we still didn't express our feelings using "I feel" statements, and we didn't listen. The arguments—over where to eat, what TV show to watch, was I too controlling, was he too inattentive—were the arguments of ordinary couples, but they flared up out of nowhere and ended not in resolution but in détentes, with him in one part of the house and me in the other. Or, more often than not, one of us stayed with the kids and the other took off, just off, away from the house until everyone was in bed for the evening.

During the early days of our marriages, a friend and I used to call these "rough patches" when they lasted a few days, a week, maybe two weeks, but this had more en-durance than a rough patch and was, well, rougher. We were both firmly convinced that the other person did not under-stand what we were going through. I couldn't see it then, but a gap had widened between us, and when we were forced to bridge it—during the holidays, on vacations, even just at a family dinner—we were hostile and irritated with each other. Kevin's habit of falling asleep in front of the TV had gone from the occasional night to most nights. A few years earlier, I would've gone down in the night if I woke up to check the kids, and brought him back to sleep beside me, but I no longer bothered. When he'd come home, often later than he'd said, I'd go out, ostensibly to exercise, write, take a break from motherhood. The truth was that it was tense when the four of us were together. It was better if one of us was gone.

The day before the split was also the first day of the autumn quarter at UW. The class I taught met in the late afternoon, so Kevin came home early to pick up Natalie and Jessie from school. We agreed he'd make dinner. I came home around six, excited from class, feeling the optimism that the beginning of the academic year always inspires, looking forward to a family dinner that I hadn't made myself. I entered the house and a feeling of hopelessness washed over me. It was a complete mess—backpacks and shoes strewn everywhere, the kitchen a jumble of dirty dishes and food left out on the counter, toys all over the living room. It wasn't as though the house never got out of control during my watch, but I was certain—and maybe Kevin was just as certain that this wasn't so—that it happened far more often when he had the kids. Besides the mess, there was an emotional chaos that I was also certain had something to do with him. Kevin was shouting at Jess, who was pouring a huge pool of barbecue sauce over her chicken from far too large a container. Natalie was yelling instructions at Kevin. On the table was a pot of Kraft macaroni and cheese with a wooden spoon lodged in it, and a nearly full gallon of milk with its cap off. In my mind's eye, I could see with crystal clarity the jug tipping over and the white waterfall of milk cascading onto the carpet.

I was both very annoyed and acutely aware that my position was essentially indefensible. He had, after all, "made dinner." I felt I should be grateful, but I was angry that everything was so chaotic and that he hadn't made a greater effort to make a nice dinner for me on the one day I worked. I knew it wasn't easy to keep a semblance of order, get dinner on the table, and keep the kids reasonably content. But, years ago, he'd often have a beautiful dinner made, complete with a pot of tea, milk, sugar, and teacups on the table. That felt like a long time ago now.

I sat down and asked about everyone's day through clenched teeth, trying to keep my feelings to myself. I listlessly ate a few bites of the macaroni and cheese. It was cold, and I wasn't hungry. The kids were long finished, so I cleared the table and started loading the dishwasher.

"What's wrong with you?" he asked, zooming in beside me at the sink. This was very unusual. He was more the sort to let matters blow over. In retrospect, I wonder if he was goading me into an argument that would give him a reason to go out.

"It doesn't matter."

"What's this big attitude about?" he asked, glaring at me with an intensity that I'd rarely seen in him until recently.

"I don't want to talk about it," I said, scraping macaroni and cheese off a plate. "The kids can hear us."

"It's okay for them to hear conflict resolved. This is all just part of life." He was standing between the sink and the dishwasher with his arms folded. I wanted to ask him to move, but I was afraid. I was vaguely aware that I'd never felt this fear with him before. Some part of me knew something was wrong, but I couldn't name it.

"I don't think we ever resolve anything. But okay. Here it is. I was disappointed you didn't make a nicer dinner." As soon as I said it, I wished I hadn't.

"I rush home from work, pick up the kids, take care of them and make dinner, and you come home complaining that it's not good enough."

"This is why I didn't want to say anything." Suddenly, holding my head up and breathing felt like far too much effort.

"You always have this specific idea about how everything should be. I don't say anything when I don't like the dinner you make."

"I just don't think it's too much to ask on the one night you make dinner that it's nice. I make great dinners for you," I said, tossing the silverware into the dishwasher with a big clatter.

"They're not really *for* me. A lot of times I come home

and you and the kids have already eaten and there's just a plate wrapped up for me."

I could see this was going nowhere. We weren't really fighting about dinner. It was about not feeling important to each other, and that was a problem we'd tried repeatedly to fix, without success. We were both getting angrier, and the kids could definitely hear us. Also, there was something surprisingly aggressive in his approach that scared me. Normally the tedium of our discussion would've caused him to back off, but that night he was becoming increasingly agitated. Now I know that it was the guilt from his spiraling debt that fueled his hostility, but all I knew then was that he wasn't the person who'd once tried so hard to understand my point of view.

"So what was wrong with dinner anyway?" He started in again.

"Well, for one thing I don't like macaroni and cheese."

"You're impossible! You really are. You can put the kids to bed. I'm going out," he said. A minute later he was out the front door.

Only later would I realize where he had gone.

A YEAR AFTER OUR SPLIT, WE'RE BOTH STILL CERTAIN THE other doesn't appreciate us enough, but we're no longer married and never have any of the good times that restore goodwill after a series of tiny injuries, and so the rift between us has widened into a chasm. Communication between us ranges from remarkably cooperative to coolly distant to openly hostile. When we come together to do the work of co-parenting, sometimes it goes so smoothly it looks like we could be running workshops for divorced parents, and other times it feels like we're coming close to making the local news. It's a complicated and tricky process, like cold fusion.

Several times each week, we flirt with danger as we shuttle the kids between our cars, our houses, and our lives. The transfer is the hardest thing to do right. I hate the transfer! The kids are inevitably wound up. It's a flurry of soccer cleats, shin guards, dirty laundry, school papers, and lunch bags flying, to the soundtrack of a terse, grunting conversation with a person who'd just as soon never see you again. Usually, before the dreaded moment, I break into a sweat, my heart starts to race, and I start madly cleaning, as if an orderly house will soften the blow of the impending chaos. I try to breathe. I say to myself, These are my children and they are coming home.

The worst story I've heard about the transfer involves a divorced couple who meet each other in a McDonald's parking lot at a designated time twice a week. After the cars pull up side by side in the lot, the children are instructed to go into the restaurant bathrooms and change into a set of clothes that belongs at the other parent's house. This story scares me to the quick. Maybe because I know a little of what it's about, how the parents don't want to deal with each other at all, don't want to see each other's houses or discuss why Suzy's socks didn't come home. But as much as

Kevin and I may not want to deal with each other, the kids *have* to go from one house to another, each week moving through the wind tunnel from Dad's car to Mom's door, popping through the wormhole from one set of rules and emotions and into another.

I remember reading an interview with Melissa Etheridge after her split with her longtime lover. She said that her lover had simply moved into a house on the property right behind hers and they let their children run freely between the two houses. I think Melissa Etheridge might be slightly more evolved than I am. Kevin just moved one block from my house, and that's a little too close. If I look across the street as I make a right turn at the end of my block, I can see his house. I try not to look.

Sometimes it feels more like "divorce lite" than real divorce. Instead of falling asleep in front of the TV downstairs, he falls asleep in front of the TV in his house just down the street. Instead of arguing in the kitchen about whose turn it is to do what, we argue in my front yard for the neighbors to hear. I'm still the one who reminds him that today is basketball practice and he is still the one who trudges into my basement to find out why the tub drains at the rate of a glacier melting. It's the result of twelve years of interdependence, of me never getting my car's oil changed and of him never washing a scrap of laundry. At the auto repair shop, my car is still listed under his name, and each time they say it, I can't be bothered to correct them, so it will probably always be under his name. Recently, on one of our better days,

Kevin asked me to explain how laundry was separated and which loads were to be washed at which temperatures.

Besides our incontinent old dog, we share a decrepit lawn mower with an impossible pull cord, which, try as I might, I can't start on my own. So Kevin starts it for me and I then walk it down the block to my house with the motor running. Sometimes people pass me on the sidewalk and look at me funny, and then I raise my head a little higher and stride right by, the way the kids and I do when they're going down to Kevin's for the night with their little red rolling suitcases in tow. Sometimes I picture myself as a character from Gloria Naylor's *The Women of Brewster Place,* determined and unapologetic. Other times I think I'm a middle-aged woman pushing a running mower down the street or a woman walking one minute with children and a few minutes later alone.

We've done things right and we've done things badly. We sign all the Christmas presents from Mom and Dad, and we back each other up. If one parent says no, the other one holds the line. But we growl at each other, and I know I have a tone of perpetual irritation when I talk to him on the phone, even if the kids are within earshot. Sometimes he makes cutting remarks, and sometimes I roll my eyes at him.

But the day our dog, Coco, was put to sleep, we did have the wherewithal to join forces to hold an impromptu good-bye ceremony for her. We stood in Kevin's front yard with our delirious dog, barely alive, lying in a large plastic file box. Each of us laid a blowsy pink dahlia on her brown shaggy fur and said why she had been a good dog for us. Natalie's friend Miranda had slept over the night before, so she joined us, too, and said how she remembered the first time she came to our house and met Coco, how she'd known from the very first day what a good dog Coco was. Kevin talked about the day he'd brought Coco home for the first time. Before there was Natalie, before there was Jess, there was Coco, and Kevin and I had loved her together. We had taken her out that night on a long walk together, out the dirt road across from our house, far into the desert, Coco out in front and the two of us side by side, taking turns holding the leash.

Sometimes our disjointed life works and sometimes it doesn't. Once, during a good patch, Kevin and I were helping Natalie to decorate her room and she said spontaneously. "It makes me happy the way you guys get along so well." Once, a long time ago now, in a very bad patch, Kevin yelled at me so loudly out on the sidewalk about whose turn it was to take the dog that a drunken neighbor wrongly assumed the situation was dangerous and called the police. When the police came, the three of us were on the front porch. I scanned the street wondering which neighbors were home and what they must think.

The two officers talked to the girls to make sure they were safe and then they asked them to go inside.

"Do you think you're in any physical danger?" the male officer of the pair asked me after the girls went in.

"No, not at all," I said, hoping he wouldn't notice the

shame burning on my face. I wanted him to think I was handling matters well, that I was a good citizen, person, and mother. "It's just a difficult situation to work out sometimes."

"I understand," he said, and looking at him, his blue eyes fixed right on me, I was pretty sure he did.

We talked for a few more minutes, but I was eager to get back inside to the girls. I knew they must've been incredibly freaked out, and I wanted to reassure them.

I went inside and called for them and we all climbed on my bed, the place we often end up when the three of us need to talk. Natalie lay on her side, her head resting on her forearm. I could smell the cherry scent of children's shampoo rising from her hair. I asked them if they wanted to talk about how they felt when the police arrived.

"I just talked to Natalie about this in the backyard," Jess said. "*Privately.*"

I heard Jessie's message: Parents can't be trusted right now.

"That's the thing about sisters. You two are having the same experience with the same parents and you can share that with each other," I said carefully, and then, looking at their blank, bewildered faces, I knew I was going to have to go deeper, acknowledge their pain more fully. "There were times my parents hurt me and the one person who really understands is Aunt Kat Kat because we both have the same mother and the same father."

Natalie brightened, propped herself up on an elbow. I

knew what had brought her back into the world—I'd finally named the truth, that their dad and I have, in fact, hurt them.

"How did your parents hurt you?" Natalie asked.

"Lots of ways."

"Name one," she demanded, and Jess inched closer, eager to hear what I'd say next.

I thought about it for a minute. Did they hurt us? Suddenly the usually handy list of injustices suffered seemed to have disappeared.

"They hurt us by raising Kathy and me apart from each other," I said at last.

The simplicity of this statement woke me from a lifelong slumber of denial. I always knew that going through life without my father had shaped me in myriad subtle and obvious ways. But suddenly I realized that the toll of my parents' divorce was larger than anyone in my family had ever been willing to admit. I'd lost my sister and she'd lost me. And the saddest part was that my parents never acknowledged that they'd taken from us something that was rightfully ours.

"On purpose?" she asked. "I mean, did they do it to hurt you?"

The question startled me. "No no no, of course not. But it *did* hurt. Sometimes parents do things and say things that hurt children without meaning to, without wanting to."

"And you've talked to Kathy about this?"

"Yes," I said. "*Privately*. Just like you two. And it has helped. It's helped a lot."

· · ·

IN THE 1950S, NOAM CHOMSKY ARGUED THAT A CHILD does not learn language through repetition and rote memorization, the way an adult acquires a second language, but possesses instead an innate ability to acquire language. Chomsky also believed that children are wired with a universal grammar, a set of rules about language that allows the child to generate new and original sentences, so that even if the child knows only a hundred words, he is able to recombine them according to those rules to create his own meaning. My sister, who moved to Mexico at the age of eight, swallowed Spanish down like a pill and woke up a few months later— her life in California an eternity away—running down the cobbled streets chased by the village kids calling her new name: *la huerita,* the blond girl.

I began French classes at thirteen, the exact developmental age when Chomskyites say the "critical period" for language acquisition ends, when a child can no longer effortlessly absorb a language, but must labor to attain it, word by word, forever weighed down by an accent. I studied the same French lessons over and over for years; I recited *je m'appelle Jean Cluny* so many times, I was pretty sure I *was* Jean Cluny. But my French classes never yielded up the great harvest of French I had dreamed of, the baguettes and loaves of language I could break apart and offer to strangers on the street. I never have listened to adult, native-speaking French people conversing at a normal speed and said to myself, "Ah, I know just what they're saying and just what I'll say."

I have spoken French slowly to French children who lost interest in me quickly once they realized I could never answer their questions with anything more than the canned responses I'd acquired from my *Parlez-Vous Français?* textbook. I have also spoken French with two Italian railroad workers who were trapped with me in a deserted station some hundred kilometers from Pisa. In France, I have spoken in French only after rehearsing sentences like lines in a play, hoping no one would know how hard I'd worked for them and how foreign these words felt in my mouth, the metallic aftertaste they left. In France, I can only express the simplest parts of myself, hunger and thirst and fatigue and the need for the check, nothing of ideas and experience fused together, just flat, declarative statements. And if all I can say is *Je suis fatiguée,* I don't know if I want to say anything at all.

It really does seem like the "critical period" is long over on this cold Saturday morning here in my continuing-ed Spanish class. I'm hacking away, turning my father into *mi padre,* hoping to learn the question that will help me unlock the mystery of my sister's childhood when I go down to Mexico next month with Markos. The Spanish translation for "Is Señor Gomez in the export business?" doesn't feel like it will be the magic key, but I persevere, conjugating verbs sloppily, tripping over my *rs* like a gringo, forgetting it all almost as fast as I learn it.

Today we're learning to ask questions, to invert our subjects and verbs and insert interrogative adverbs—*cuándo, quién, qué, dónde, por qué. Por qué* sounds so gentle, so softly inquisitive, compared to its demanding English equivalent *why*. Maybe if I could've used *por qué,* I'd have spent more of my life asking the hard questions I've avoided entirely too well. *Why?* Why did you do that? Why did you leave me? Why did you gamble away all you had? Why did you leave Kathy in a convent in Mexico? Why didn't *somebody* bring her home?

I've spent my whole life telling people that I don't know what happened. My parents divorced, my father inherited a chunk of AT&T stock, he bought a ranch in Mexico, and when he didn't know what to do with his nine-year-old daughter, he boarded her in a convent. There you go. Don't ask me why. It's a mystery.

The thing Chomsky's theories can't explain is how a child can rearrange her words to ask a question if she's never told that such a question could exist, if she thinks the world might break in two with the utterance of the single syllable *Why?*

I'm on the phone with my mom again. She's in her house in Olympia, and I'm in mine in Seattle. Circling around the questions I most want to ask, I ask her once again what happened when she told my father she was in love with another man.

"He'd never, ever hit me, but he asked me if I loved him and when I said yes, he slapped me so hard the string of pearls I was wearing broke, and the pearls scattered all across the hardwood floor."

I catch my breath. *String* of pearls? We've been over this.

This is the stuff we know. It was a pearl *earring*. He slapped you so hard the pearl *earring* you were wearing skittered across the floor. Remember it sounded like a hard pea? Remember the echo of the solitary pearl?

I say nothing. How has she gotten this wrong? If she no longer knows it's a single pearl earring, she won't do any better on the questions she couldn't answer a year ago, but I continue, a little listless now, "Can you tell me how Kathy left?"

"Jack told me he wouldn't give me a divorce unless I gave him Kathy."

This is news.

"So he got Kathy from the beginning? She never came to live in the apartment after the divorce?" Kathy's version of these events, of leaving JoJo's house in Redwood City in the night, is falling into question, along with my Richie Rich and Dr Pepper version of the same events.

"No," she says. But then her voice grows noncommittal. "I don't think so."

Her memories of this are weak from lack of use. Until my own divorce, I never asked any of these questions, and I still can't ask the ones that put her on the spot. They bloom in my mind, and then close up again. They always start like this: *"Por qué . . ."*

WHEN I'M GOING THROUGH TERRIBLE TIMES, MY MOM always likes to say, "This too shall pass." It's unbelievably irritating. Sure she means well, and of course there's loads of wisdom in the saying, but when I'm in something hard that isn't going away, I'd prefer solace that doesn't remind me that the problem probably won't end until right near the time when I can withdraw from my 401(k) without penalty.

Maybe it's just a hair easier to say "This too shall pass" if you've never co-parented. Since my kids started shuttling between Kevin's place and mine, I think I understand just a little better why my father moved so far away with my sister and why my mother let him. It has finally occurred to me that my dad didn't want to face the woman who loved another man more than him every Wednesday evening and every Sunday morning. He didn't want to discuss dentists and piano lessons and report cards with her. I'm sure he wouldn't have wanted to add back in the cost of the co-pay and then divide the child's medical bill in half and then have a tense little phone call with my mom about it. If he couldn't have the life he'd known, he wanted a completely new one, free of anger and hurt and compromise.

When I go to Mexico and see his house in Amatlán de Cañas, surrounded by rolling hills of scrubby bush and skinny cattle, I say to Kathy, "Okay, I can see moving to Mexico, maybe Puerto Vallarta or Mazatlán, but why *that place?*"

"I think," she says, "he was trying to get as far away from Mom as he possibly could."

And maybe my mother was okay with him nearly dropping off the face of the earth, even if he did have a daughter in tow, even if the fifty-dollar Wells Fargo checks with my father's scratchy signature and a stagecoach rumbling across them didn't come very often, even if she had no one to call if she couldn't pick me up from school or if I had a fever and she had to work. She had her own life, her own business, her little bungalow, her convertible—a life that no one could touch, a life that made her pretty happy.

With my mom, I grew up without the rules or schedules that seemed to dominate the "real" families, the ones with a dad. The lives of my friends looked exhausting: the catechism lessons, the table setting, the sighs of annoyed mothers, the baritone of fathers lowering the boom. Why, I wondered, did these parents appear so frustrated with their mostly obedient children when my mother was so blindly pleased with me, a child who never participated in any of the chores or lessons these children suffered through? Their parents watched them so closely: math tests retrieved from book bags for review, television snapped off quickly after *My Three Sons,* bathing suits promptly hung to dry after swimming lessons. I doubted I could live up to this rigorous standard. There was something soft in me, some slackness of spirit. I'd lived outside the kingdom for too long and was spoiled from too many dinners of Ritz crackers and neapolitan ice cream. I knew my friends possessed some intangible and powerful wisdom about creating an ordered kingdom of one's own they'd no doubt be putting to good use a few years down the road.

In 1969 my eldest sister, Susan, had a hippie wedding in

the backyard of our California bungalow. There were big Day-Glo pink and yellow flower-power flowers all about the yard, and the guests swallowed dots of acid and gulped pink champagne. Susan was the picture of hippie-beautiful in eyelet cotton and yellow ribbons, a crown of daisies. Her long, straight hair stretched down to the ribbon waist of the dress. In a stiff white minidress and patent leathers, I was the consummate flower girl. The girl any father must love.

When my father showed up—suntanned, in a white dinner jacket, smelling like Old Spice and sweet tobacco—a teenaged Kathy was with him. Freshly sprung from the convent, she leaped about our crowded house with manic abandon until her energy was spent, then collapsed in the back of my mother's convertible with a magnum of Baby Duck.

"Hello, Teddy," he said, squeezing my shoulders in the warm, easy hug of an uncle. There was no explaining of absences, no apology. He was smooth—unwrinkled, unworried. I asked him then if he'd come back for my wedding day to give me away, too. "Of course," he said.

I walked slowly down the aisle, clearing the way for the bride with my face cast down into the tight bouquet of daisies. This was the only day since my infancy that all the people I called family were gathered in a single place. There would be no more days like this.

I'D PRETTY MUCH PICTURED THIS TRIP AS STRETCHES OF mind-blowing sex interrupted briefly by deeply rewarding mornings of detective work that would unearth startling information from my family's past. Sort of *9½ Weeks* meets *Indiana Jones*.

But since we've landed in Puerto Vallarta, it's been a bit more like *Who's Afraid of Virginia Woolf Takes a Holiday*. We've bickered over who has the room key, where we parked, whether we should eat dinner now or later (Now! Has he forgotten that I'm hypoglycemic?), why I'm giving large-denomination paper pesos to the toll taker when we could be using up all this perfectly good change, whether it was morally wrong to give the beggar woman on the beach in Sayulita an American dollar, and whether it's a good idea to drive 20 kph over the posted limit on backcountry roads when we're in a country where one of us knows only the word *gracias* and the other knows only phrases such as *Señor Gomez trabajo* in *el business* of export.

It doesn't help matters when I think of how much finagling it took to pull off this trip. I'm as tired of the "it takes a village" saying as the next person, but it certainly applies this week. Almost everyone I know is helping to make this trip work. Trish, Anika, and my friend Jenny are all taking shifts and have copies of the master schedule that includes school, dance classes, playdates, and the times to deliver Natalie to the Safeway to sell Girl Scout cookies. Anika (who, by the way, has a real job during the day) will stay with the kids two nights and then hand them off to my mom, who will stay two nights midweek, and the last three nights they'll be with their dad.

Markos, whose daughter lives with his ex-wife, is only a shade away from being completely oblivious that I'm maxing out every favor account I have so that we can have this child-free vacation. The night before we left, I'd just finished writing out turn-by-turn directions for my mom from our house to every strategic point in the neighborhood and was stuffing a week's worth of lunches into paper bags when he tried to coax me out of my exhaustion by saying, "Be happy. Tomorrow we'll be in Mexico." I almost lost it.

But relations begin to improve now as we finally arrive on the outskirts of Etzatlán, which apparently no citizen in the province of Jalisco has ever heard of, and which is—we can now confirm—a five-hour and not a two-hour drive from Puerto Vallarta. Despite all my obsessive pawing of the map, we still missed the turnoff for Etzatlán and had to retrace our route until finally a nice local guy pointed us down the right dusty street.

We roll down the windows and breathe in the dry, warm air and the raw scent of the earth. It's twilight, and the landscape of irrigated fields and yellow hills is fading as we enter the town of adobe houses painted matte turquoise and rose. Occasionally a donkey clomps by, making its deliberate way down the brick-lined streets. We drive toward the middle of the town to the plaza flanked by the cathedral where Kathy once sat on Sunday mornings, listening to Spanish and Latin in her schoolgirl uniform, her light blue eyes sometimes glancing up at the bleeding Christ above her. This is the same plaza my mom arrived at in 1964 when the cabdriver brought her here from the Guadalajara airport. She sat here on one of these white iron benches and showed the passing school-girls a picture of her blond daughter. The girls squealed, "*Sí, sí, Catalina,*" and then ran down the street shouting until my sister came streaking out of an old building beside the cathedral yelling, "Mother! Mother!" When I finally asked my mother, "Why did you leave Kathy there in Etzatlán once you'd found her?" this is what she told me, "She was in Jack's custody, care, and control."

The next day we check out of the Cadillac Hotel, the same hotel my mom stayed in forty years ago, where the cockroaches skitter across the floor as soon as the lights go out and even after they are snapped back on again. One night is enough of following in my mother's footsteps. We move into the El Centenario Hotel, a disproportionately grand establishment considering the modest size and expec-tations of the town. Apparently it was built to accommodate Spanish royalty who came to scope out the situation in the colonies. Judging by the surprised expressions of the owners and the tomblike quiet of the halls, it seems possible that we might be their first guests since the days of Pancho Villa.

After we're settled in our new hotel, we walk to the town plaza, with its central white gazebo ringed by old de-ciduous trees. There's a scattering of benches where teen-agers gather in clumps and old men chaw on cobs of grilled corn covered in lime and salt. We're side by side on a bench, at last enjoying the sort of idyllic moment travel magazines promise, when Markos surveys the plaza and says, "In a way I think Kathy was lucky growing up here."

"Lucky?" I know just where he's headed with this. Markos prizes over all else the quiet, simple life. This, in fact, is a common sticking point between us. I don't *like* chaos and stress, but I'm convinced there are some things, whether it's the proximity of well-stocked bookstores or the clamor of my children's voices, that make my hectic, harried life in the city worth every bit of the toll it may or may not be taking on me.

"Yes, I think so," he says. "A kid could have a real childhood here—wandering around dirt roads, chickens and donkeys everywhere. A quiet life of simple routines. Plus, the weather is perfect—sunny and dry."

"That's insane," I say. I've adopted a lot of Markos's habits of speech lately. My sentences are peppered with phrases such as "that's insane" and "it was a nightmare." He pulls off this sort of hyperbole better than I do, though; he's got that malcontent Eastern European worldview to back it up. From me, these sayings fall a bit flat, as though I'm a college sophomore fumbling around with words like *trope* and *metonymic.* "She was completely separated from her family, living in a foreign country!" I say.

"There are worse things," he says, with an air of finality that tells me this particular perception is not going to budge.

It bothers me that he doesn't rank siblings forced to live

in separate countries very high on the list of life's injustices. I want him to recognize my loss and be outraged for me, the way I've never been fully able to on my own behalf. It seems like a person who's been through as much as he has should understand why I don't think my sister was lucky, why I don't feel lucky. But his childhood seems to have prepared him to expect nothing, to meet injustices with a shrug and a "What can you do?" rather than the resolute refusal to accept the unacceptable that I want him to have.

Outrage about the ravages of your lover's childhood is, to me, *de rigueur* in love. I've certainly taken on as my own the drama of his childhood. My childhood memories have made a second home in dreary, Cold War Budapest with its bombed-out buildings and crackling soundtrack of Radio Free Europe. The problem, of course, is that they're not my own memories. And, because they're not, I don't understand exactly why he insists that happiness can never be more than an ephemeral shadow. In short, I want to pull down his bleak Eastern European nihilism brick by brick. I want to prove to him that people aren't always *that* bad, that humanity isn't on a course of total destruction, that the good people are still a neck ahead of the bad and the race isn't over yet.

But even if the world *is* overrun by evil and menace, couldn't we just have a good time today? I've sat on a romantic beach with this man and listened to his account of Russian trappers forcing a group of Aleuts to jump off a cliff to their deaths in a frigid sea. I've danced in the living room to The

Clash while he's shouted over the music about gangrene and diabetics losing limbs. I've urged him again and again to let go and have faith.

I think a few clues to his mind-set might be found in the English-Hungarian dictionary. For the English word *nothing,* there are no fewer than ten possible Hungarian translations. For *nothingness* there are a dreary six, *nothing doing* weighs in with four translations, and the ever encouraging *to come to nothing* yields another four. I was born in California! We don't need to talk too much about Nothing! We need words for "How's the surf today?" and "Dude, try this, it's homegrown."

I think I know and understand why he's the way he is, but I also feel like his darkness could threaten the shaky foothold I've gotten on happiness. Part of me wants to forget how terribly wrong life can go. I don't want to hear any conspiracy theories before breakfast.

Yet maybe it's for his behind-the-Iron-Curtain brooding, and for the fact that he really does see the pain of the world, that I love him. When I say something that makes him smile or, better yet, laugh out loud, I'm filled with a sense of hard-won triumph, as though I've scored a personal victory in the world's debate over whether the cup's half empty or half full. And in some ways he's the one who is acutely aware of life's fullness—much more so than I. He's sure that bread baking in the oven is worth all the time it took him to make it, certain that no figs will be better than the ones he's waited seven years for his tree to yield, and he's absolutely positive that there's such a thing as true love and that I'm it.

I search my memory of the eighth grade. I find him—
the boy whose locker was just to the right of mine, a sullen
boy of fourteen, in his new-world Levi's jacket and feathered
hair, spinning through the numbers of my combination lock.
Sometimes I'd stand exasperated at my locker, running the
numbers one more time through my stubborn lock that refused to pop open, and he'd offer to help. This quiet boy I
never thought much about, he was the only one to whom
I told my secret numbers. I didn't know then why he didn't
talk or where he was from or that he'd left his mother behind in a closed country only four years before. I didn't want
to know. I was thirteen. I was a mere one step down the social pyramid from cool. I just wanted him to open my locker.

The next morning we leave our hotel with the grand circular stairways of marble and the courtyard of violet bou-
gainvillea and Moorish tiles and head north over the border
into the province of Nayarit, over the shrubby rolling hills
that will finally drop into the green valley that holds the village of Amatlán de Cañas and the house my father and sister
moved into in 1963. Today we will find that road of river
stones that leads to the house of white stucco. The house
stands but there are no solved mysteries inside, just a woman
named Sylvia and her parrot. The story returned to *el norte*
with my father years ago.

We stop at a field of silvery blue agave, half an hour out
of Etzatlán. The wind is dry and warm. The only sound is the
crunching of stones spraying out from under our feet, rhyth-
mic and reassuring as breath. Without talking, we weave our

way through the rows of the dusty blue cactus that wind around this rocky hillside. Markos is a little farther up the hill now, taking photos of cactus and the curves of the horizon, and I feel a comfort in his quiet, occupied presence.

I try to name this feeling of peace and melancholy, this acute reverence for both life and death. I've felt this before—wandering through an abandoned graveyard in the Santa Cruz Mountains, climbing up the ladders of the Anasazi cliff dwellings in New Mexico, feeling at once both the power of each breath you take and the generations who have breathed and lived and loved before you. I imagine my father driving past this same hillside, on his way to visit Kathy at the convent school in Etzatlán. He'd have been in one of the Buick convertibles—white or starlight blue—that he'd driven down from California. He'd have had the top down. Maybe he felt full of purpose and direction, or maybe he felt like he'd thrown away all he knew to be good. Maybe out of habit his fingers moved to the radio buttons before he remembered that he'd moved past where voices could reach him.

I've come all this way to find out something I'm still not willing to know. When Kevin and I first split up, friends would ask me, "So when did the gambling start?" "Where did he go—casinos? Card houses?" "So when did it start exactly, what set him off?" Good questions, each and every one. Questions to which most people in my position would demand answers. But each time I was on the verge of asking him, a wave of fear washed over me, and I said nothing.

Once he told me the name of one of the card houses

where he lost some of the money, but for the life of me, I can't remember it now. Sometimes when an errand takes me down that sleazy row of car dealerships, box stores, and card houses on Aurora Avenue, I'll ask myself, Was that it? Or was it that one?

Even after we were split for good, I was still too scared to know what the road that led him away from me looked like. Maybe I knew that once he told me the truth, my version would be lost to me forever. Just as I still can't say to my mom, "Tell me everything. Tell me how it happened. There's no detail I'm afraid to hear."

BUT A TIME WILL COME, LONG AFTER THIS TRIP, WHEN I will ask my mother my primordial *why,* and I will know then it wasn't just that she was afraid to tell, it was also that I was afraid to ask. The keeper of the secret was me—and all the rest of us who'd rather live without knowing than face the fact that those we love have failed us.

On this day, the truth will come tumbling out of her. She will tell me the high price of her freedom. She will rummage through cupboards and pull out old cardboard boxes and find the answers I'm finally ready to know. She will overnight me Kathy's letters from the convent, the ones dated from the spring of 1965. She will rush to me in an envelope marked URGENT the very letters that implicate my father and her of neglect, the one in which Kathy asks to be sent soap and pesos, the one in which she tells my mother how much trouble she will be in if Father finds out she has written this letter, in which he's told her that if she is bad she'll be taken to live on the ranch, where there is no school.

In the package, there is one more envelope filled with translucent air-mail paper, and here I find my mother's acknowledgment of what Kathy and I lost. I know my mother's seen it and she knows I've seen it. To compose this letter, Kathy used every resource she could pull together—a pencil, her rudimentary written English, guilt, and the art of the ultimatum—to ask in loopy cursive for one big favor, a favor that my mom and I both know was never granted:

> *Mom, if you would please do a thing for me. I want to see Teddy and for Teddy to see me. It can only be two days but I WANT TO SEE TEDDY. It's important. I know you're going to say that you can't do it but if you love me, you will bring her. If you don't love me you won't bring her and if you bring her, bring her before 1 month.*
>
> *Love,*
> *Kathleen*

MARKOS AND I SIT UNDER A BLANKET ON THE ROOF OF our hotel, where, the brochure tells us, *generalissimos* once slept during the Mexican Revolution. We watch the sky darken from pale blue to pewter to black, the lights of Etzatlán pop out one by one, and then the full moon's rise across the tender desert sky. The air is warm, soft with gentle wind, sweet with the scent of flowers with names I'll never know. In another lifetime, it might've been a moment to which I surrendered. I might've felt all other moments slip away and my focus zoom in to just this: the ancient light of an indifferent moon and the eyes of a lover who wants only me. Rapture would've been just an instant away, its promise as real as the cool, smooth tiles beneath us.

In this lifetime, I feel the pull of the moon, but I also feel an equal force, one of resistance; it's the one that keeps me here with two feet on the ground. I've had my moments of passion, yes, but mostly I've been the child who stayed up waiting for the lights of her mother's car to illuminate the driveway with the force of a giant moon on a clear night, the one who stood guard even when the need for vigilance was long past.

I look up. I see the moon—white and full and perfect. I see us momentarily from above: the white stucco walls of this old hotel, the two of us huddled under this blanket, the wind from the west growing stronger. But then the image splits in two. Yes, I'm right here under this Mexican moon with my boyfriend. But I'm also still back at home, under this same moon in my overgrown yard, in front of my falling-down house, beside my two daughters who need me.

13

The Year of the Rat

I could see that I was moving through the stages of the divorce recovery process I'd read about. I was long past Shock and Denial with its hibernation and raw pain. Adjustment with its attendant ambivalence and coming to terms with the new reality of divorce was behind me as well. In many ways I was in that period referred to as Acceptance. I was feeling a sense of belonging and comfort in my new life just as the book had predicted. But had I skipped the phoenix experience? What happened to the moment of magical redemption that supposedly capped off Adjustment and ushered in this new king, Acceptance?

There had been no shaking of sooty ash from golden wings, no soaring triumphantly from the ruins of my life into something undeniably new and profoundly better. Part-time work had evolved, piecemeal, into something more. I was teaching writing groups several times a week as well as a class for the university extension program. I was on a budget and still paying for my own health insurance, but at last self-sufficient.

I had a boyfriend who shared a few wonderful nights and days with me each month, but mostly he was in Canada living the life he'd begun years before we reunited, and I was in Seattle giving all I had to a family I'd started more than a decade earlier with someone else. He made me happy, but he wasn't the answer to all my problems.

I'd made a few new friends who were around my age and single through widowhood, divorce, or default—creative, talented women who were living amazing lives on their own. Long coffees and walks around the lake with these women became the backbone of my week, feeding my resolve to make a life that made sense all by myself.

I started going to yoga a few times a week and witnessed all those beautiful left hands—some brown, some white, some ringed, some bare like mine—shooting up like arrows toward the ceiling as each of us breathed into triangle pose, into the moment, into our lives, whether they be solitary or coupled.

I began to write again and to dig up weeds and plant dahlias, lilies, sweet peas, and roses, and I began to see my family not as broken but as altered.

All this happened as slowly as learning a new language. It was all gained piece by piece, word by word, punctuated by moments of anger and despair and big clumps of loneliness. There was no day like the one I'd hoped for, the day when I'd think, Wow! See how everything has worked out for the best! In short, there was no phoenix.

But there was a rat, and I now think that this scrappy bottom-dweller was an envoy from the animal kingdom who'd come to shepherd me into my new good life. In Chinese astrology, the rat is considered a sign of good luck, and although I didn't see it that way at the time, I think in my case it might be true.

Like my other troubles, my rat ones began with a protracted period of denial. I had made so many excuses for the problems in my marriage and kept them so well hidden from myself that I hadn't seen the truth even when it was right in front of me. This new relationship was no different. The bottom corner of the cereal box stored by the basement door had been torn off "somehow." Damaged in the store, perhaps? Yes, that's it, and that's why Raisin Bran had fallen onto the white carpet. There were flecks of black dirt that looked like wild rice on the basement stairs. I told myself it was just something the kids had tracked in. When at last I was ready to admit that maybe, just maybe, it wasn't dirt, I was only able to commit to calling it "mouse poop." Like a nice family in a cartoon, we had—oh dear!—a mouse. Eek! One. Small. Mouse.

I tossed mousetraps for my little friend into my cart at the grocery store and nudged them down between a box of cookies and a box of laundry soap. I plotted how these plastic, enclosed traps would lure my opponent through a teeny, tiny little mouse hole to a yummy hunk of poison bait. With the dead mouse neatly entombed, I would then collect the trap, deposit it swiftly in the garbage can, and slam down the lid. Problem over.

The only flaw in my plan was that no little mouse ever made it as far as the bait. And I didn't dare think it was because the boy was too hefty to squeeze himself through the designated hole.

One day I chaperoned Jessie's Brownie troop on a field trip to a pet store. As brown-vested girls streamed around me, darting from fish tanks to hamster cages, I nonchalantly plucked a booklet from the rack, *Caring for Your Rat*. I looked at the cover photo—the flat, soulless eyes, the glistening fur, the teeth like sewing needles—and shuddered in horror, repulsed down to my toes by its essential ratness. Breathing in the stench of urine-soaked wood shavings and dried kibbles of food, I leafed past "Feeding Your Rat," "Playing with Your Rat," and "Cleaning your Rat" to "Types of Rats."

There he was, my nemesis, black and disgusting: the Norwegian Rat. I skimmed past the sordid details of his lineage and zoomed down to the line, "This rat loves basements." Yes, that's him, I thought.

I entered the next phase of our dysfunctional relationship: the shame and the cover-up, interrupted by occasional backsliding into denial. Could it be that coming out about rats was harder than coming out about divorce? I didn't even think I could tell Trish. Surely she'd never want her daughters to play at our house again. I wasn't ready to admit to the outside world that I was a single mom with a rat (rats? *no!*)

in her basement. What if we became known as the "rat house"? I wasn't willing to fall *that* far from middle-class grace. I'd deal with this problem quickly and quietly, and no one would be the wiser.

At my neighborhood hardware store, I threw a few sundries in my basket—masking tape, screws—and scanned the rows for rat poison. I felt criminal and creepy, like Joan Crawford in *What Ever Happened to Baby Jane?* I skulked around the aisles, but the stuff was nowhere to be seen. Maybe you have to ask for it, I thought. Like the girly magazines, maybe it was kept behind the counter.

"Excuse me," I whispered to the clerk at the register, "I'm looking for rat poison?"

"We had some, but we're all sold out," he said in a booming voice.

"Sold out?" I said, in a low voice.

"What you whispering for? You don't think your neighbors have rats? All these houses around here"—he waved his hand in every direction like a compass—"I don't care how fancy, they have rats."

"No, they don't. I mean, they can't. It's not possible. I've never heard anyone say they had rats." I wasn't ready to believe that all this infestation was happening without so much as a sotto voce mention.

"Well, it doesn't look like you're telling too many people, either," he said, and turned to attend to the next customer in line.

It was true. People might talk about sexless marriages, a

husband's pot habit, or even their children's OCD routines, but never had I heard any of the women at school, or even a trusted friend, utter the word *rat*.

Alternately comforted and deeply repulsed by this new knowledge, I walked to my car with images flashing before me of rats tearing through basements, slinking up drainpipes, and rappelling down through nursery windows. Suddenly this genteel neighborhood was transformed into a grimy underworld governed by packs of Norwegian rats—a bunch of Scandinavian hoods holding the jogging-stroller set at their mercy.

I stopped at another store and obtained the needed poison. Averting my eyes from the gruesome image on the box, I planted it in all his favorite haunts. He ate it—flurries of the stuff strewn all over the carpet in the grim aftermath—and then seemed to live a fuller, more robust life because of it. Traces of him all over the basement (*not* wild rice) served as a constant reminder of his victory. I told Kevin about it, and he came over and placed a freakishly serious poison (in child- and animal-proof containers) in strategic locations outside, and cut all the ivy away from the house.

The problem vanished. Presto. I was free again and ready to forget that the whole nasty business had ever happened.

A few rat-free months later, my friend's son, Dylan, and Jessie were downstairs going through the dress-up clothes. Suddenly I heard Dylan scream, and before he could even fly up the stairs I knew my troubles were back. I spent the next twenty minutes debriefing Dylan. Not only had he seen the rat, he had seen it so clearly the image was emblazoned on his brain. He could've picked this rat out in a police lineup. I offered him chocolate-chip cookies, told him incessantly how sorry I was, and asked him every four minutes whether he was okay.

Then the phone rang. It was Dylan's mom. The saving grace was that I know her very well and we like each other. It wasn't just a random mom of some random kid who'd come over for a playdate. But still.

"So I'm thinking I'll pick Dylan up at five. Does that work?"

"Yes, that's good. They're having a good time, but there is something I need to tell you. Something happened."

"A car accident?"

"No, not that." I felt bad about all the horrible atrocities that might be running through her head, but it still took me a minute to spit it out. "Dylan saw a rat. In my basement."

"Oh, that's not that bad."

"You don't think? I mean an honest-to-god rat inside my house."

"But rats are from the natural world. It's not like something completely foreign to him."

"Right, the natural world, which is usually *outside*. Not dashing by the dress-up box!"

"Okay, don't worry," she said. "He'll get over it."

Maybe Dylan would get over it, but I wouldn't. I didn't want to go through life afraid of my basement. Even if I got an exterminator, I could never be sure the problem wouldn't come back. It was an old house with lots of the little holes and crevices a rat loves. I'd had it with "old-world charm" and the pressure of keeping an old house together with very little income. It was time for a change.

A week or so later I was visiting a friend who lived in a new town house in my neighborhood. I asked her what she'd paid for it, assuming it was a lot, given the gleaming hardwood floors and functioning plumbing, and I was surprised to find that my old and funky house was actually worth more. Lots of people wanted a turn-of-the-century farmhouse in a quiet area to renovate—married people with two incomes or money in the bank or a general handiness. A few days later I started dropping by town-house open houses, picturing us living in a little less space but with everything new. A place with nothing to repair and as tight as a fortress.

I'd thought of moving before, but two factors had kept me put. First, I hadn't wanted the kids to have to go through another change right after the divorce, and, second, I didn't see how I could use another Realtor when my ex-husband was a Realtor in the very neighborhood we lived in. It seemed illogical not to give the business to the hand that paid the child support, but if we worked together, he would be in my house and in my finances, and we would be talking to each other several times a day.

Logic won out. One day I was picking up the kids from Kevin's, and I told him I wanted to look for a new place and asked if he would help me. That afternoon he, Jess, and I went and saw a couple of places. It was as though he was any Realtor and I was any single mom looking for a house, except that Jess called him "Dad." The next week he called me, excited about a new listing. It was the one——three bedrooms, a gas fireplace, hardwood floors, a yard big enough to garden but not unmanageable, and *no basement*. I knew the girls and I would live a new kind of life in this new place, one in which Mom wasn't cussing as she pushed the mower over the unruly lawn, or figuring out why the bathroom door wouldn't shut, or dodging rodents to do the laundry.

The next few months were a chaos of cleaning out the house and packing for the move. Kevin and I enjoyed a temporary reprieve from our roles as exes, and relaxed into a coolly professional relationship. He treated me like I was any other client. If I asked him to update the pictures on the website or to change a detail in the listing's description, he got on it right away. When I was speaking, he listened and then spoke. There were several tricky moments during the negotiations, and each time I was impressed with how he handled them. I started to remember more of his good qualities that I had forgotten.

When it came time to clean out the basement, Kevin offered to help. We attacked it together, both with gardening gloves on, tossing stuff for the dump or Goodwill out the window. I remembered how well we'd worked together side by side in the early days of our relationship, how I'd admired his energy and willingness to do whatever it took to get the job done. Occasionally, one of us came across some memorable item from the past—a doll belonging to one of the girls, a Halloween photo—and called the other to come see. But mostly we tackled the big mess, which felt right because it was a big mess that we had mostly made together.

And then it came—the last day we would live in the house we had moved into as a family, the house we'd found after Jess's first birthday party at Salmon Bay Park. The old hawthorn tree in front of the house had been in full bloom the day we first visited, shooting branches studded with pink blossoms across the sidewalk and into the street. "This feels like our house," I'd said to Kevin, and four-year-old Natalie had bolted out of her car seat to say, "But we haven't seen the inside yet." A few days later we did see the inside and it was, in fact, our house.

The three of us stood in the driveway looking at our old house. This was the house where Natalie had cartwheeled for the first time, where Jess had built fantasy worlds under a sheet suspended between two dining room chairs. The house where my heart had broken and had been made whole again.

We took turns saying good-bye. Natalie talked about her lavender room and the day she saw it for the first time. Jess thanked the driveway for all her days of scootering there. I looked at the house one last time—the high pitch of its roof, the windows trimmed slate blue, the little front porch. "You kept us safe and warm. Thank you," I said, and we drove to our new house and our new life.

. . .

I WISH I COULD SAY THAT OUR GIRLFAMILY LIFE IS FREE OF strife, that I've struck the perfect balance between the need for money, my commitment to be there for the girls, and my unabating desire to be engaged in a grown-up exchange of ideas and energy. I wish I could say that my girls had a mother who didn't get raggedly tired and that the stress of keeping three lives in order didn't pound my patience to a brittle crisp.

It's undeniable that there are dozens of moments each week when two parents could probably do with relative ease the tasks I find nearly impossible: managing two kids doing homework at the same time, saying good night to two kids at once when one is afraid to stay in her room alone and the other desperately needs five minutes of undivided attention. If we were a two-grown-up household, maybe I would make pad Thai for dinner and the girls would learn to like it or not, and maybe they would have the chance to interrupt an adult conversation about interest rates or the shortsighted-ness of city planners. They would learn grown-up stuff. As it is, I often eat hamburgers and garlic fries and the one chicken and pasta dish they both like, and occasionally *I* interrupt their blow-by-blow accounts of the latest Nickelo-deon show to command them to chew faster so I can deliver them to their dad's before I go to work. In a two-parent life, Natalie could've stayed home and gone to bed the night Jess smashed her finger in a door, instead of sitting bleary-eyed in the hospital waiting room until ten-thirty on a Sunday night.

Back in the two-parent days, there was a meditation I

sometimes did before I went to sleep at night. I'd focus on an image based on a silver pendant necklace Kathy had given me for a birthday—an abstract design that depicts four figures, two big and two smaller, presumably a mother and a father and their children. The four figures form a sort of ring-around-the-rosie circle. Since the pendant is made out of one piece of silver, the characters are not welded together— they are one. What unites them are the outstretched arms of each figure. It's not just the children dancing, and the parents up in the bleachers cheering them on. The parents are dancing, too.

This was my dream of family, a group that comes together to dance and allows each member to spin out into the world and orbit back again. This is still my dream. I still work to create a home life that is a circle that supports each of us as we go out in the world to do our individual dances. And I know this is still Kevin's dream, too.

Mostly the girls and I come together in ordinary ways. We join hands to say grace at the dining room table or dance in the living room to an old funk song like "Car Wash" or walk together down the beach at Golden Gardens and get ice-cream cones after dinner. Once in a while we unite for something spectacular, like Jess's belt ceremony at the martial arts studio or a visit to JoJo's ninety-two-year-old sister, Pat, on the North Shore of Oahu, where enormous sea turtles live on the beach. Sometimes we're driving down the highway listening to a book on tape together, and I realize how cozy it is and take a glance in the rearview mirror at

Jess sniffing her blanket and Natalie dreaming out the window. We are a family, and a mostly happy one.

When Kevin and I first split up, I used to think that if it weren't for the kids I'd never see him again. That would be that. He would go his way and I would go mine. We would have the sort of all-or-nothing divorce my parents had. And sometimes I still admire the simplicity of that idea, just as I'm awed by the pristine lines of Frank Lloyd Wright. But mostly I don't wish for the "clean break" because, as much as Kevin and I have hurt and annoyed each other, he's still the person who was the primary witness to my life for more than a decade. He is the person who knew me as an insecure young woman starting a teaching career, and as an insecure new mother, and as an insecure writing student, and eventually as an insecure writer. He wanted the best for me through all those years, as I wanted the best for him as he went from young student to social worker to Realtor. After we split up, we were very angry with each other. We both believed that we had been in some way betrayed. We both went through periods of thinking the other person was the source of all our troubles. But I don't think there was a time when either of us stopped wanting the best for each other. We'd been involved in each other's stories for too long; we couldn't help but want to see each other succeed.

If I had been able to walk away, it would have been easier. I might have been less angry, less annoyed, less frustrated over the last few years. My life, I'm sure, would have been cleaner. But I'm not sure it would have been better.

. . .

It's real girlfamily craziness here in the new house this morning, maybe a premonition of the teenage years when the soundtrack of morning will be the constant whir of blow-dryers and we'll be in and out of one another's closets looking for borrowed sweaters and shoes. We're all running up and down the stairs of our tall, skinny house in search of panty hose and hairclips and safety pins, all except for Markos, who's lying as low as possible, ironing and re-ironing his new white shirt in my bedroom.

We've been preparing for this day with shopping trips, dress fittings, and a full-scale dress rehearsal, but it's like a natural disaster—no amount of preparation can prepare you for the day of a wedding in which you're a bridesmaid and both your daughters are flower girls. Actually, Natalie is a junior bridesmaid because she looks a lot more like fourteen than eleven, and I'm the maid of honor and I feel a lot more like a matron than a maid.

My friend Anika will marry a good man today. In seafoam and ivory, we will clear her path, spreading hope and white hydrangea petals in our wake. As much as I joke about my status as the world's oldest bridesmaid, I'm glad she picked me for this role and that it doesn't seem to her like too much of a bad omen to have a single mom and her kids emerging on the first strains of Bach's "Jesu, Joy of Man's Desiring."

We finally make it into the car unscathed, and I realize that after all my fretting, we're going to be absurdly early. I look at my daughters, who suddenly look to me like young Kennedy children in their ivory dresses and matching sweaters and tiny handbags and dyed-to-match shoes. Natalie's damp hair is pulled into a demure twist, and Jess looks like a genius with her new short bob and her round, blue-framed glasses. Okay, I think, somehow I'm pulling this charade off. We look more together than we actually are, but it's all good.

Now that we're on the road, I'm looking forward to seeing my friend Jenny at the wedding. She lives in L.A. now, and I haven't seen her for a few years, since before her divorce. She will be there with Andy, and it will be the first time I've seen them together as boyfriend and girlfriend. Andy, Jenny, Anika, and I went through graduate school together ten years ago. Jenny and I were the two married moms, and we got together to talk about writing and whine about motherhood while our kids ran all over the park or her big living room overlooking Lake Washington. A year or so after me, Jenny got divorced as well, and we whined long-distance about parenting plans and the trials and tribulations of divorce. Last year she found a job she really liked, and now she and her old friend Andy are planning to get married. I talked to her a few days ago on the phone. It's the first time she's sounded truly happy in a long time.

I haven't been to a wedding since the divorce, and I'm bracing myself for a sudden rush of melancholy. But even with the exquisite yellow light illuminating the altar of the darkened chapel and the brilliant sound of the piano breaking the hush, no scary feelings jump up to greet me. I look through the crowd and see Markos in the back, and, closer to the front, Jenny and Andy sitting with her young daughter and son between them. I don't wish it were me getting married. I don't wish I were still married, and I don't wish that I had never married. I have the sort of objectivity of mind that I imagine is common to accountants and lab technicians. I'm proud of my daughters. I'm happy for David and Anika. Yet as simple as it is to be happy for them, I'm surprised that I'm not feeling more of a tug on my heart as they face each other to say their vows and exchange rings.

And then the minister says to the friends and family gathered here, "As David and Anika say their vows to each other, you might want to reach out and put a hand on the arm of your partner, recommitting yourself to them."

I notice David's parents touching each other gently. And then, behind David's parents, in one of the front pews, I see Andy's right arm—easy to pick out in its striped seersucker suit jacket—graze the heads of Jenny's children to hold her beautiful shoulder. It's such a simple act of love, a triumph for the craggy kind of love that can grow between cracks in the sidewalks, and for joy after adversity.

On my first, eternally long nights alone, I slept firmly entrenched on my side of the bed, the left-hand side by the window with the view of the gnarled, ancient hawthorn tree and—on very clear days—the strange, ghostly white triangle of Mount Rainier. Kevin's side had been by the door, presumably so he could ward off intruders and guide in children seeking warmth on a cold night. Some nights—with the four of us in here—this king-size bed was barely large enough, and I slept with one arm dangling, ready to break my fall if I were pushed off the edge.

Then, some months after the split, I conquered that space as vast as the Canadian Prairies known as the middle of the bed. I climbed in at night and positioned myself in the very heart of the bed, patted my pillow down, and splayed out my arms and legs into the void that had once reminded me I was alone. In the next, rather odd, phase, I slept horizontally, flanking the pillows that lined the head of the bed, pressing myself into their solidity, half-believing that I wasn't alone, that some omniscient, loving presence was cuddled next to me.

Now this is just my bed, and I've learned how to sleep here alone. The distance between Markos's house and mine seemed to lengthen as the obstacles between us multiplied. Our visits grew further and further apart until, at last, the relationship ended. I can't forget, though, how he cared for me as a girl and as a woman and how he stood beside me in court the day my divorce became final. He made me feel loved when I felt unlovable. And because of all this, I'll continue to think of him as part of my inner circle even if we're no longer together.

Some nights I wake up in a panic over money or the children's psyches. I turn on the light and stew for a while and then I read. I marvel at how my light disturbs no one and I can read as long as I wish. Then it occurs to me that if I weren't alone, I wouldn't be up in the night trying to calm myself down with a book.

Other times I lounge in bed talking to friends on the phone (there *are* some advantages to being single!). I was talking to my friend Christina the other night. She's on the verge of a divorce herself. We talked for a long time about the divide she and her husband can't seem to bridge, and then she asked me if I'm happier now. Part of me wanted to tell her that I am. I'm happy! The water's not that cold! Jump in! I wanted to give her hope of a better life. And I wanted to have made *progress*. I wanted to tell her that I'd had my phoenix moment, that I'd arrived at a place of steady contentment.

But I also wanted to be honest, so I told her, "I don't know if I feel *happier,* but I feel *real-er*."

Of course, she wanted to know what that meant, and frankly so did I, so we fumbled through it together, the way you can with good friends. And what I think it means is this: I feel as though my middle-aged shell has been blasted off me. I may not like what I feel sometimes in this post-divorce life, but I do know what I'm feeling, and I prefer this knowledge to the constant confusion I felt at the end of my marriage. Even if I have to hear myself whine—I'm tired, I'm lonely, I'm broke—at least when someone asks me what's wrong, I don't gaze into the distance and say in a wispy voice, "Oh, nothing, really."

Divorce has returned to me the rawness of spirit I had as a girl—the girl who was disconsolate when her canary died, who snuck out the window to see her boyfriend, who slammed the fridge door, opened it, and slammed it one more time when she didn't get what she wanted. She was the girl who stayed awake to watch the shooting stars on a velvety August night, sprained her ankle jumping for joy in the school library, and memorized all the lyrics of Joni Mitchell's *Court and Spark*. The girl who begged friends to bowl just one more game.

Acknowledgments

I want to thank all the people who've supported my writing over the years. To name a few: Jennifer Niesslein and Stephanie Wilkinson at *Brain, Child* magazine (thanks for publishing me first), my favorite writing teacher—David Shields, Ted Conover (Because of a long chain of events that you set off, this book came into being. Thanks!), Maya Sonenberg, Daniel Jones, Linda Bierds, Christina Adams, Paula Temple (hun!), Nicole Aloni, Bill Litwin, Trish LaGrua, Thomas Mihalik, Sheila McBurney, Nancy Gillies, Chris Gordon, David Candy, Jocelyne Mange, Lauren Burns, Jenny Fan, Andy Gottlieb, Jenny Daves, Sara Rubenstein Kenney, Sarah Harwell, Frank McCourt, Antonya Nelson, and all my writing students at the UW Extension Program (the cliché about the teacher learning from the students applies here in spades).

Anika Nelson Bavas has given my writing the kind of care and attention writers normally reserve for their own work and made an enormous contribution to this book's editorial process. I am grateful to have such a smart and generous friend. My boyfriend, Kent Miller, gave me the sort of support the single mom/writer dreams of—well-timed chocolate, smart edits, and rides for my children to the movies, Starbucks (don't ask), and martial-arts class. Lucky me!

My family has also been a huge source of support. My daughters and my ex-husband have trusted me enough to express my version of this part of our family's story. They have their own stories, and I hope they know that I understand and honor that. Thanks to my mother, sisters, and brother, who've all cheered me on.

Many thanks to my agent, Dan Lazar, for watching out for me every step of the way. Thanks also to Lucinda Bartley and Mary Choteborsky at Crown, who were helpful throughout the process. And heaps of gratitude to my editor, Rachel Klayman, for her tremendous insight, intelligence, and indefatigable interest in the welfare of this book. I'm honored to have worked with someone who cares so much about the craft of writing.

Reading Group Guide

QUESTIONS FOR DISCUSSION

1. Every divorce is challenging in its own way, and many of Theo's circumstances were unique to her family. Which aspects of her situation and which of her feelings are most likely to be universally shared by people who separate or divorce?

2. How might the narrator's experience resonate with women who haven't been through a divorce?

3. *Kirkus Reviews* wrote that "Women going through the pain and turmoil of separation and divorce will appreciate Nestor's candor and wit." How do you think men going through divorce would react to this book?

4. At the end of Chapter 5, the narrator says of her husband and herself, "The forces that would keep us together for twelve years and those that would tear us apart were already in place, invisible to us but quietly and constantly at work." In retrospect, have you ever observed that the qualities that first drew you to a partner or even a friend were the same qualities that later caused a rift in that relationship?

5. The narrator's mother plays a prominent role in her story. What challenges might her mother have faced as a divorced woman in the early 1960s? Do you think the author's own divorce changed her relationship with her mother?

6. In Chapter 3, Nestor writes, "When I wore my wedding rings, I was a different person, emboldened the way you can be in a Halloween costume. I could laugh as loud as I wanted and go out with dirty hair and sweatpants. I was married! I belonged. Someone loved me and it showed. I could reference a husband to a new friend or a store clerk. They didn't care if I was married or not, but I did. My ring said, You can't touch me. It was like base in a game of tag. I was safe." Are married people somehow "safe"? Are they treated differently from single people? Is there still a stigma in being a single woman over a certain age?

7. Many states require divorcing parents to attend a seminar about how the divorce might affect their children. What do you think Theo got out of her experience with the one she attended? Do you think these seminars are helpful?

8. At the end of Chapter 11, Theo and her daughters discuss Theo's new relationship in a scene that culminates in her older daughter, Natalie, tearing up a leaf that symbolizes her parents' marriage. How do you think children's experience of divorce differs from adults? What are some of the ways you've seen children express their experience of divorce?

9. Why do you think the author is drawn to Markos? Are there people in your life who have kept a hold on your heart?

10. Ultimately, the relationship between Theo and Markos does not work out. Does their breakup give you insights about the conditions under which a couple, once they've broken up, can ever get back together?

11. One of the most emotional moments in the book occurs in Chapter 12 when Theo travels to Mexico to visit the town where her sister was raised after their parents divorced. How did your opinion of Theo's parents change after reading this chapter? How did your opinion of Theo change? Why is reading the letter from the narrator's sister, Kathy, a turning point for the narrator?

12. Theo begins to claim the king-size bed for her own by sleeping in different spots on the bed. What are some things you have done to reclaim your sense of yourself after a relationship ends? What did you discover about yourself in doing so?

13. What does Theo ultimately learn about herself (or others) that she might not have learned if she'd remained married?

14. How would you describe the author's voice and use of language? Do you think she found the right balance between humor and sadness?

15. Compare *How to Sleep Alone in a King-Size Bed* to other memoirs your group has read. Do you think the author discloses more or less of herself than other memoirists? Are there aspects of Theo's life you wish she had written about in more depth? When did you most identify with her?

16. The book divides the divorce recovery process into three stages: shock and denial; adjustment; and acceptance. Do these three stages resonate with you? Have you experienced these stages in your own life—either after a divorce or some other loss? Would you subdivide the process further?

17. By the end of the book, the narrator is in a distinctly different place in her life than she was in the first chapter, yet the changes she makes are very gradual and take place over the course of a few years. Can you compare her experience to a period in your life when you made a life change in small steps?

If you would like to arrange for Theo to speak to your reading group, e-mail her at theo@theopaulinenestor.com.